The Psychology of
Transformation in Yoga

Vaidya Atreya Smith

This book was first released in 2002 under the title *La Psychologie de la Transformation en Yoga*, published by Editions Turiya, France.

Revised and corrected July 2013

Other books by Vaidya Atreya Smith:
Prana the Secret of Yogic Healing, Samuel Weiser, 1996
Practical Ayurveda, Samuel Weiser, 1998
Ayurvedic Healing for Women, Samuel Weiser, 1999
Secrets of Ayurvedic Massage, Lotus Press, 2000
Perfect Balance, Avery Publishing, 2001
Ayurvedic Nutrition Course Textbook, Editions Turiya, 2001
Pañcakarma - Shodhana Chikitsā Textbook, Editions Turiya, 2003
Dravyaguna for Westerners, Editions Turiya, 2009
Ayurvedic Nutrition, CreateSpace, 2010

www.atreya.com

ISBN: 1490972064
ISBN-13: 978-1490972060

DEDICATED TO SRI H.W.L. POONJAJI

Sri Harilal W.L. Poonja is a disciple of the renowned saint Sri Ramana Maharshi of south India. Sri Poonjaji lived 7 years with Ramana from 1942 to late 1948. Sri Poonjaji is best known in Europe though the writings of Father Henri Le Saux (or Swami Abhishiktananda) where he is referred to simply as 'Harilal'. In the USA he has become known in the 1990's primarily through the teachings of Andrew Cohen and a woman called Gangaji.

Sri Poonjaji is a mystic of the highest order living the non-dualistic, or Advaita Vedanta, path of the classical Indian spiritual tradition. His ability to live this traditional teaching and not simply intellectualize about it was so remarkable to the priest Father Le Saux that he devoted several chapters to him in his famous book of the 60's, *Secrets of Arunāchala*. Another aspect of interest for the Western reader is that Sri Poonjaji is married and the father of several children. This offers a far more practical and accessible vision of classical Vedanta than is normally given by monks or swamis.

The teaching methods of Sri Poonjaji are direct and often abrupt. He is adamant that the Divine Consciousness, Atman or Self is everyone's real nature. This 'Self' is always present and is readily available to each person at any moment; no practice is needed to realize the Self. He faithfully continues the same uncompromising teaching tradition of his Guru, Ramana Maharshi. Sri Poonjaji went into Mahasamadhi on September 7, 1997 at the age of 87 in Lucknow, India.

CONTENTS

vedic? Ayurveda?

Note: all chapter head quotes are from the *Avaduta Gita*.

1

INTRODUCTION

*"Some prefer to be non-dualists while others prefer to be dualists. Neither of them truly knows the Absolute which is devoid of duality and non-duality."*1.37

This is the first English edition of this book which I wrote between the years 2000 and 2001. My agent tried unsuccessfully to find a publisher for me in the USA, and then Great Briton in 2001. As this book is not oriented to the general public no publisher was interested to print it as it is not a book for the mass market.

At the end of 2002 the French translation of this book appeared on the market where it received a small but positive reception. It has sold consistently to those people passionate about Indian culture over the last eleven years. Therefore, it is with great pleasure that I present the revised and corrected version of this book, in English for the first time. For those of you who have seen various versions of it in the past, notably students, this is a 'definitive' version with a number of details corrected or revised and dates reflecting this updated version. Herewith, I present the original introduction.

After studying several of the ancient Indian sciences over the last forty years I believe a vast misunderstanding exists today regarding the fundamental vision on which these disciplines are based.

In the process of teaching these sciences over the last twenty five years I have observed that modern people generally have great difficulty to grasp the essential differences between the ancient Vedic Indian thought and present day conceptual thinking. This modern tendency of conceptual thinking is confined to defining the world we live in through psychology and the intellect. This is a fundamental error when applied to the Indian sciences. Additionally, this modern tendency is not limited to the West or other geographical locations – few Indians can now grasp the enormous difference between ancient and current perceptions. As the whole world, East and West, moves towards a more materialistic, psychological orientation this is, perhaps, to be expected.

The purpose of this book is to explain another way of perceiving the world that is not psychologically based, but rather experiential. I call this approach "The Psychology of Transformation According to Yoga." This book begins by explaining the most fundamental concepts of the Samkhya system in simple terms and then analyzes how this Yogic vision of creation transforms our everyday life. The approach of this book is neither historic nor intellectual; rather it is a practical and experiential one.

In this book I am presenting my own understanding and experience of the many talks that my teacher gave during the early 1990's. It also includes my practice as a health care professional for the last twenty-five years and as a teacher of Ayurveda for the last nineteen years. If there are mistakes they are mine and not my teachers. For most of the early 90's I was living in India absorbing the

Samkhya by osmosis. This still remains the primary teaching methodology between students and teachers of the traditional sciences in India today. Therefore, one can say that the approach of this book is existential rather than intellectual.

Present conceptual thinking is strongly dominated by an individualistic, psychological approach that is founded on a mechanical vision of reality. Using the ancient Indian sciences from this 'mechanical conceptual approach' has little value. The only value – and that is invaluable – of using the ancient Yogic sciences today is to understand the deeper meanings of life and to help humankind to find happiness, health and peace here and now. That is the purpose of this book.

The Psychology of Transformation in Yoga shows us how to live life with good health through Ayurveda and Yoga. It shows us the function of time and how to observe when different periods are beneficial for specific activities through Jyotish (Yogic astrology). Yet, first and foremost it is a practical system for our daily lives.

The Psychology of Transformation in Yoga reveals the hidden meanings of life, death, the soul, happiness, health, astrology, esoteric sciences, kundalini, karma and reincarnation - to name a few. Practicing any of the Indian sciences like Ayurveda, Yoga or Jyotish (astrology) without deeply understanding the "Psychology of Transformation" will cause these disciplines to be presented in a cerebral, static manner. This is a disservice as the higher aspect of these studies is lost and they become vulgarized. However, when the deeper purpose of Yoga is revealed these same practices help lead humanity to health, truth, happiness, peace and real knowledge – the knowledge of who we are.

2
SAMKHYA AND THE PSYCHOLOGY
OF TRANSFORMATION

*"Everything in this universe is filled with the Absolute. And
since the Absolute is covered by Itself (the creation) how can I worship
that formless, indivisible, immutable Supreme Beatitude?"* 1.2

I met H.W.L. Poonjaji in early August 1991. I had
bought a small book written by one of his disciples in
Amsterdam two weeks before when I was in Europe. Prior
to that moment I had never heard of Sri Poonjaji and his
message that 'enlightenment is here and now' and not
some event in the future.

From the small book, which told the story of how an
American met Sri Poonjaji in India, I had the choice of
three cities in India. These three cities were the only
indication I had of where to find Sri Poonjaji in a country
of almost a billion people. Yet, within 24 hours of deciding
to find him my two companions and I were virtually
thrown to his door in a new suburb of Lucknow, Uttar
Pradesh, India. My first reaction on entering the bare
concrete living room was of my good fortune. There were
only eight other people present in the room that morning

and we were welcomed warmly even though we came in the middle of a meeting. Having spent the last ten years in a large ashram with thousands of fellow disciples in West India I was happy to see so few people, yet this was not what stirred a sense of good fortune in my awareness.

On entering the room I saw that I was with an enlighten being – one of those rare humans who has ceased to identify themselves with their own body and personality. In spite of the current marketing of enlightenment and instant realization there are actually very few awakened beings on the planet – certainly not the ones traveling around saying they are realized souls. I spent the next week trying very, very hard to become 'instantly enlightened'. I asked Poonjaji a number of questions relating to the functioning of the mind, effort, practice, healing and meditation. Up until that time I had been meditating for fifteen years. Until the summer of our meeting I had been spending an average of three hours per day meditating. I had been practicing a number of breathing methods in Yoga (pranayama) and had also spent the last five years doing Vipassana meditation for an hour each morning. My main interest as a healer had drawn me to work intensively with pranic currents in the body through breath.

However, in spite of more than fifteen years of spiritual practice I was both dissatisfied and disillusioned with my 'progress'. This is why I was grateful to at last meet a teacher I could have close dialogs with about my inner transformation (or lack of). At that time I did not know that Poonjaji was called 'the butcher' by a number of people in Europe in the 60's and 70's for his ability to cut the ego into pieces. I was a bit difficult so it took 'the butcher' ten days to dispel my doubts and intellectual mind. In that moment of illumination 'I' ceased to exist and what remained cannot really be described, yet is totally familiar as my own 'Self' or the real 'I'. The identification of the body and mind where stronger at that time, however, and after a wonderful five days of bliss the false 'I' of psychological identification arose to claim the 'experience of unity' as its own experience.

There followed a period of intense loss and depression as I realized that I had thrown away a jewel simply because of a basic habit – identifying with the body / mind functioning. I spent the next year learning why this habit of thinking of myself as limited to a personality had dominated over the substratum of pure consciousness that is every human being's true nature. As I sat for several hours each morning five times a week for the next year listening to Sri Poonjaji I began to understand the nature of creation as seen through the psychology of transformation. The movement of consciousness through creation is called the Samkhya and was a vision from the ancient Vedic times given by the Rishis or Yogic seers. I didn't know it at the time, but I was being taught Samkhya on a daily basis.

I learned the intimate functions of the thinking process and how emotions are dependent on its functioning. I learned this not through an intellectual process but by experiencing the depth of psychological pain. I passed through both the mental anguish and physical pain that accompany the loss of deep-seated concepts. I had months of migraine headaches as my body was purified from past emotional indulgence which is considered normal in the West. Slowly I learned to develop that lost quality and attribute of the mind – discrimination.

By summer of 1992 I thought I had understood enough of the 'I' to leave India and return to Europe and begin to live a normal life of working, paying bills and being generally stressed out. I reasoned that the only way to discover if my state of peace was due to re-identification or the peace silently radiated by my Guru was to return to the 'real' world. It took about seven months to realize that the peace I was experiencing was due more to my teacher than my ability to change completely the habit of identifying with the mind / body functioning.

I returned to Lucknow in north India in 1993 to try and see what I not understood correctly the previous year. I then spent another year in almost daily sessions listening to my teacher. The primary subject of these sessions was always to discover who or what our real 'I' is – and by that encounter of 'Self' see what remains. During this year as with the previous year I spent with Poonjaji I had a number of revelations of Self or the true 'I'. This was a common experience of people who came to see Sri Poonjaji. He was known to have the gift to still the mental activity of the seeker – by his presence alone. The seeker then discovered his/her own nature of Self, or 'I', underlying the mental functioning.

After more than a year I again wished to test myself in the fire of modern living to see if the peace of Self was indeed something borrowed. That was at the end of 1994 at which time I moved to Paris and began a new relationship which became a happy marriage and remains both peaceful and happy to this day. During these last years there have been many difficult times and a number of problems in which to test pervious concepts and habits. In conclusion, I am happy and I am no longer searching for anything. I no longer have a spiritual practice, nor do I meditate in the sense of daily sittings. My stream of thoughts is there and often is very disturbing to the psychological functioning. I am the same as other people around me and have no special state, gifts or intelligence. I feel that my experience is not unique. However, my relationship to the psychology and body is very different. Strangely I am totally transformed from my contact with Sri Poonjaji and find it difficult to articulate that transformation in words.

This transformation can be understood as the psychology of Yoga, or union. It can also be described as Samkhya – an experiential path of transformation. The Psychology of Transformation provides a practical, logical method to first understand how we as humans become incased in the habit of identifying with the mind / body functioning. Second, it puts this knowledge in the context of the universe. Then finally it returns us back to our original face – pure beingness or the 'I' that is consciousness itself, or Self.

Through some strange process of default I have begun to explain this system to a number of people over the last nineteen years while teaching Ayurveda. I can say from my own experience that if used as a system of transformation our lives are altered and ones vision of the world changes for the better in a profound and meaningful way.

Vaidya Atreya Smith

3
AN EXPERIENTIAL APPROACH TO TRANSFORMATION

"Be aware of the Absolute always. It is continuous and everywhere the same. You say, 'I am he who meditates,' and 'The Absolute is the object of meditation.' Why do you divide the indivisible?" 1.12

What is the 'system of enumeration' or *Samkhya Darshana* that forms the basis of the Psychology of Transformation in Yoga? First of all Samkhya is not a philosophy, which presents the primary problem in using the system. There is no actual term that can be used to explain what the Samkhya Dharshana exactly is – hence, the common translation of 'system of enumeration' or the order of manifestation. This meaning is close to the actual Sanskrit word Samkhya. The word Dharshana means literally "to see". A loose translation of Samkhya Dharshana could be: "The direct observation and experience of manifestation in a logical, linear and progressive manner in the entire universe, known or unknown to promote transformation of consciousness."

For lack of any better term modern scholars in both

the East and West have attached the word 'philosophy' to the Samkhya vision of transformation. This is indeed unfortunate as it represents the fundamental error of modern conceptual thinking to try and grasp the existential reality of existence. Samkhya is a 'Dharshana' or way to perceive reality. Nature, en gros, or in totality, is a kind of 'Beingness' that is in a constant flux of change and interrelationship. To attach the word 'philosophy' to 'Samkhya' commits a grave and serious error that is extremely hard to rectify. Philosophy can be described as: "The use of reason and argument to seek the truth or knowledge of reality (concrete or abstract) that results in a set of beliefs based on the previous lines of reasoning."

The Samkhya system is based on 'observation and experience' while philosophy is based on 'reason and logic'. Therefore, trying to understand the Samkhya through reasoning or philosophy will cause the thinking individual to miss the most important aspect of the system – that it is existential by nature. The only way one can truly approach the Samkhya system is through experience. And the only way this kind of experience can be gained is with some framework of knowledge or through a teacher. However, an ordinary teacher will not be able to help. This requires a teacher who can actually help the student experience the 'beingness of reality' and not just intellectualize about the possible 'cause of manifestation'. Unfortunately, this kind of teacher cannot be found in the Universities and seldom in the monasteries or ashrams throughout the world.

Why should any modern person even care about understanding Samkhya in the first place? One main reason is that over the last century much of the ancient Vedic and later Hindu knowledge has been filtering into the Western world. Yet few people practicing Ayurveda, Hatha Yoga, Tantra, Raja Yoga, Laya Yoga, or Jyotish (Vedic astrology) really understand the basis of these disciplines. Furthermore, terms like Chakra, Kundalini,

Dharma and Karma have all been taken out of their proper context and largely misunderstood. The context of all these terms and disciplines is the Samkhya system. It explains clearly how the creation manifests along with the individual human soul. It explains in detail how the mind comes into being and how it becomes disturbed and often ill. The Samkhya gives a new meaning to our present life on earth and our true purpose here.

There is a tremendous need to approach individuals from a deeper level – one could even say a spiritual level. If the practice of Ayurveda, Yoga and Jyotish miss this orientation then they become mechanical in their use and application and they are no longer 'holistic'. As a culture we do not need more 'natural' or ancient mechanically based systems. If we are going to use a mechanical system the modern biochemical approach to the universe and medicine works fine. However, we do have a great need for deeper applications of a true 'holistic' approach both in health care (Ayurveda) and in astrological counseling (Jyotish). Yoga is actually the practical application of this - though today is has come to mean just the physical postures of health care.

Particularly in *Vedanga Jyotish* (the Vedic 'science of light' or astrology) there is a tremendous need for the spiritual background of the Samkhya system. If this is missing then the astrological counselor becomes little more than a fortune teller or new age 'psychotherapist' – both of which have their place in the grand scheme of things, but which are already filled by various Western practices.

How then can we understand the 'deeper meaning' of the Samkhya? First we must look at what we call knowledge itself, as there are two kinds of knowledge. Understanding a subject or system intellectually is useful in school, work, and other daily activities that comprise much of our waking time. However, intellectual understanding, philosophy and other mental activities have little power to bring happiness or peace to an individual. Hence, on a fundamental level there are two forms of knowledge – one learned and one lived – intellectual or experiential.

The Samkhya system recognizes three ways to receive knowledge:

1) direct experience - *Pratyaksha*
2) inference - *Anumana*
3) verbal or textual testimony - *Aptopadesha*

Inference falls between experience and testimonial knowledge.

Once we begin to approach life and actually live it we are all confronted with the reality of our knowledge and understanding of life. This is very much like learning math in high school and being confronted with actually balancing your checkbook when many of the checks have not yet cleared the bank. The actual practice is different than the theoretical knowledge obtained in a learning situation. Additionally, the bank account is always changing as our financial interests grow. Therefore, modern experts on intelligence use adaptability to judge how intelligent a person is, not memory.

The adaptability method teaches the student a subject in one context and tests the same student on the same subject under completely different circumstances. This requires mental flexibility, adaptability and creativity on the part of the student who must now apply what he has learned previously in a new situation. This applies the intellectual knowledge so that it can become experiential. Once the person has had the experience, or is living the experience, it can truly be said that they understand the subject.

Imagine studying all about Africa, the flora, fauna, diverse cultures and geography. When you have accumulated enough of this information you pass exams and start teaching others. Until this knowledge is put into actual experience – in this case going to Africa – the information is just second hand. It is not the person's actual experience, but only heard or read about in a testimonial manner. Imagine another person who does the same study and then goes to live in Africa for 10 years. Who will be the most interesting teacher or dinner guest? Who actually has the experience of what Africa is like? Who now has a synthesis of both intellectual and experiential knowledge?

I know people in Europe who teach Ayurveda, the Indian system of natural medicine, and have little or no practical experience with patients. They teach without having the years of working with clients and facing a number of different individuals with unique problems on a daily basis. I know yoga teachers who teach different postures without the least idea of why these postures where developed and how they need to be applied to different types of people. I know Indian astrologers who are quick to tell you that your marriage will end and that you will lose all of your money simply because these are their own fears and conditioning.

When using any of the ancient Indian disciplines – whether for personal or professional use – it is important to understand the foundation on which all these topics are based. The Samkhya provides not only the basis for these disciplines, but it is also an experiential system that gives real knowledge of life. Without the use of Samkhya in an existential way the knowledge remains second hand and therefore inferior to a more complete, or holistic approach.

The modern tendency is to address Samkhya intellectually and most writings on the subject are dealing with second hand information. From an existential point it is irrelevant that the ancient Vedic *Rishi* (literally 'one who sees reality directly') Kapila is credited with first putting the Samkhya into a systematic form. Additionally, it is also irrelevant to refer or use the main text of the Samkhya system, the Samkhya Karika. The approach of the present book addresses Samkhya through experience and my own encounter with my teacher, Sri H.W.L. Poonjaji, who passed away in 1997. Therefore, the serious student may find deviations from classical works on Samkhya.

This, however, does not present a problem. The Samkhya is very broad and there are many ways to understand it, even classical texts do not agree on many points. This modern presentation will hopefully be useful to clarify some subtle points of the system and indicate its use as a transformational method in the modern world.

Technically the Samkhya is the system that explains, step by step, dimension by dimension, how the universe is created – not only 'in the beginning', but through every moment of our lives. This is why it is called the system of enumeration. It is the 'daily process of creation' that produces responses or 'karma' in our lives. And it is also this same 'karma' or result of the 'daily process of creation' that binds us to the cycle of time and space.

One of the fundamental ideas of Samkhya is that the whole universe is interrelated on all levels. The current popular dictum, 'macro and micro cosmos' comes from the Samkhya system. There is an infallible logic to the system. If something is stated to work on a cosmic level then it also has to work on a micro level. The reverse is also true – the logic has to function equally well on every dimension in order to be part of the Samkhya system.

Another primary aspect of Samkhya is that of intelligence. The fundamental position of Samkhya is that the whole creation is a manifestation of conscious intelligence. Even a rock has some level of consciousness as it is irrevocably connected to the cosmic intelligence that is the basis of creation. Hence, any system of health or psychology coming out of (or based on) Samkhya must first honor the intelligent principle and work with that intelligence. *Ayurveda*, the medical system based on Samkhya, strives to work with the intelligence of the body. It promotes health through the different systems of the body and by using metaphors for the body's three intelligent principles. These are called *dosha*, and are named

Vata, Pitta, Kapha (the intelligent powers of movement, transformation and cohesion).

If the Samkhya is kept at an intellectual level then these fundamental aspects cannot be truly addressed. This is because they will remain as second hand knowledge. The Samkhya system must be experienced to be understood correctly.

Therefore, the next chapter begins with the process of creation and how it slowly manifests through the universe. When the creative process is explained we will explore how the Samkhya can be used in our daily life to bring understanding, clarity and mental peace. Then we will explore how it is possible to use the Samkhya as a practical system of transformation for the human potential to return to its own source or Yoga.

The real value of the Samkhya comes when we begin to use it as a practical methodology rather than as a 'philosophical' system. When we begin to use it as a practical method our own approach to the ancient disciplines changes and we begin to touch the more profound aspects of the systems we use personally or professionally. This is because we begin to touch the more profound aspects of our own being. When explored properly the Samkhya opens our mind and intellect to different ways of perceiving the universe. In the next chapter we will begin with the first two principles of the creation – consciousness and matter in latent or non-manifested forms.

Vaidya Atreya Smith

4
CONSCIOUSNESS AND MATTER IN LATENT STATES

"As water mixed with water remains the same undifferentiated water, so Prakriti (latent matter) and Purusha (pure consciousness) both appear identical to one who knows the Absolute." 1.51

There has never been a beginning, nor will there ever be an end to IT. My teacher called IT the 'substratum'. He referred to it as the substratum because it is before everything and supports everything – all things come out of this substratum. Nothing is before or prior to this substratum, even emptiness or 'the void' comes after the substratum. By its nature the substratum cannot be defined, described or experienced. It cannot be known. Either you are it or not - but you cannot know it. There is no in-between.

The *Upanishads*, ancient scriptures of *Vedic* India, have several names for the substratum. Some of these are: Atman, Parabrahman or Self. However, there exists confusion about these names and what they mean as they are often used to indicate other levels of creation. This is a general problem with the Sanskrit language because the context of the word changes its meaning. Therefore, if you don't understand the context of the word then you miss the meaning completely. This is also true for all of the ancient disciplines like Yoga, Ayurveda and Jyotish that are written in Sanskrit.

From the substratum arises Purusha or 'pure consciousness'. This happens for no reason. It is hard for the conceptual mind to accept that there can be an event or action without any reason. Nevertheless, this is a very fundamental point of the Vedas, Upanishads and Samkhya – there is no reason behind the creation (for example see Brhadaranyaka Upanishad, 1.ii.1 and the commentary of Shankaracarya).

"Some say that creation is for the enjoyment of Purusha, while others say it is only for His indulgence. Actually creation is the nature of Purusha for what desire can He have whose desires are always fulfilled?" Māndūkya Upanishad, āgama-prakarana, 1.9

Purusha – Latent Consciousness

Samkhya begins with the Purusha – pure consciousness in a latent or un-manifested state. Purusha is sometimes called Atman, Brahman, Prajāpati, Hiranyagarbha or Virjāt in Vedic texts. Most people are not able to make a clear distinction between Purusha and the indescribable, unknowable substratum. Purusha is not possible to 'know' either, but it has been given three qualities that are used to help understand it. Unlike the substratum (where there is no possibility to give it any quality - *nirguna*) Purusha, pure consciousness, can be given three primary qualities. Even though Purusha is indefinable and unknowable we are given the means to recognize it through its three attributes – *Satcitanand*, or *Sat* (Beingness), *Chit* (Consciousness), and *Ananda* (Blissfulness).

Purusha is that which the Indian mystics call *Turiya* or literally, "the fourth" or transcendence. According to

Samkhya there are three levels or planes of existence that manifests in a number of different ways. For example: past, present and future; hell, earth and heaven; sleeping, waking and dreaming. The "fourth state" is beyond these states or "trinity", that refers specifically to the waking, dreaming and sleep states of human consciousness. The Upanishads state that when a human transcends the three normal states of consciousness they arrive in the "fourth state" or Turiya. This is the Purusha, or pure being without name or form.

Occasionally a text or teacher will refer to another state, simply as "beyond the fourth" (*turiyatita*). There is little information on what is meant by this, but it is obvious that there is something beyond the manifestation of pure consciousness or Purusha. "Beyond the Fourth" implies that there is something beyond Beingness, Consciousness and Blissfulness. That is what my teacher referred to as the "substratum", the Absolute or Parabrahman.

Purusha cannot be talked about simply because it is not possible to describe it beyond sat chit ananda (Being, Consciousness, Bliss). All of the sages of the past have failed to describe it directly – many have become poets in some attempt to describe it. Others have chosen to remain silent as they saw the futility of trying to describe the indescribable. The only way to comprehend Purusha is to become it. In the attempt to intellectualize Purusha we miss it. It is enough to know that it is latent, un-manifested or existing as a pure potential. To try and go beyond that is to miss the point.

One other classical definition from the Upanishads and Samkhya is that Purusha is eternal – it has no beginning or end (see for example *Brhadaranyaka Upanishad*, 1.iv.1 to 1.iv.5 and the commentary of Shankaracarya and *Rig-Veda*, X.129.1-4). In some schools of Samkhya this is used to define what is reality. The logic is that if something manifests and then un-manifests it is not real. By this definition the human body is not real because it is born, grows and dies. Because of this there are several schools that declare the world to be "non-reality" or "illusion" (Maya). However, to take this literally misses the whole point of the original observation.

The emphasis is on the eternal nature of Purusha – pure consciousness – not the transient nature of the manifestation. People wrongly put the emphasis on the manifestation and declare that "everything is illusion" using this to justify un-loving behavior towards their family or friends, ignore social responsibilities, or just general selfish behavior. At the very least it causes mental deception. The school of "all is illusion" is valid provided the student understands the meaning and purpose of the teaching. That teaching is to confirm that only Purusha, that which is unchanging consciousness, is real. Why? Because it is always there and everything else comes out of it.

Another aspect of this same observation is that of "everything is consciousness". All things arise from Purusha as we shall see, hence as pure consciousness is the source of all the manifestation everything can be said to be consciousness. This is a more life positive approach while the 'all is illusion' school is a more life negative approach. These can also be defined as the "everything is empty" or "everything is full" schools.

Still another approach is that expounded in the Upanishads of 'not this, not this'. This is yet another way to arrive at Purusha. It is simply declaring that everything that is not Purusha, pure consciousness, is not IT. This is a process of negation that is much safer than the school of 'illusion', as it does not create the same possibility for mental delusion. Another way is to speak of emptiness or the 'school of the void' which says that there is 'nothing' only emptiness. Both of these are also slightly life negative as they use the methodology to negate everything other than Purusha.

My teacher was using both positive and negative methods depending on the individual he was working with. With me he used the "everything is consciousness" approach. Even the emptiness is full of Beingness or Consciousness and therefore full.

The reason why there are so many different approaches is that Purusha is unknowable. In an effort to help people try to return or merge into Purusha the ancient and modern sages have tried to describe it in as many ways as possible. Often a sage may insist that the approach they are teaching is the only way. There can be several reasons for this, however, the Samkhya system allows for a diversity of explanations.

"That Purusha who is ever-present, consciousness and pure goes on creating charming objects for the senses even when they are asleep. Purusha is Brahman, Purusha is called the immortal. All worlds are fixed on Him, none can transcend Him, He is That." Katha Upanishad 2.2.8

Prakriti – Latent Matter

Purusha cannot manifest anything because it has no qualities that are related to matter. Being unknown it is devoid of the potential to manifest. Therefore it needs a partner to manifest itself. Without a partner Purusha remains latent as pure beingness. In Samkhya the next principle of creation is called Prakriti, latent matter, or potential matter.

Samkhya states that Purusha, for no reason, begins to reflect on itself. From this process of reflection Prakriti (latent matter) is born and begins to interact with Purusha (consciousness). All of this happens simultaneously, the reflection of pure consciousness on itself, resulting in latent matter, which then begins to interact with its source, pure consciousness. Hence, the 'play' or interaction of pure consciousness and latent matter is the fundamental cause of the manifestation. It has no reason to begin, nor does it have any goal. The Upanishads say that there is no goal of the creation other than for Purusha to experience itself. Being alone (mono) Purusha cannot know itself, as that requires two (dual) to exist. Hence, with the arrival of Prakriti dualism comes into being.

From Prakriti onwards knowing is possible, understanding is possible. Before Prakriti arises understanding is not possible – only existential being is possible. Prakriti is the actual source of the material manifestation. Prakriti is feminine in nature and is often referred to as Nature itself. In our language we could call Prakriti the power of Mother Nature. In Sanskrit another name of Prakriti is *Sakti* – the pure, latent, creative energy of creation. Sakti is feminine in nature as it has the potential to create the whole universe.

One metaphor that is used to explain Samkhya is the use of the masculine and feminine principles. This is represented by the deity archetypes of the later Hindu gods *Siva* and *Sakti*. Both pure consciousness and the pure energy of creation can be traced back to the earliest scriptures of ancient India, the *Rig-Veda*, as different archetypal energies (For example the Vedic deities Rudra, Agni, Surya, Indra, Vayu, etc.). In these metaphors the masculine and feminine principles are used to illustrate the union of two opposites. This is easier for us to understand due to the sexual experience humans have. However, it is important to realize that metaphors are used to teach and help the student understand something that is actually beyond understanding.

By taking this allegory too literally it is possible to miss completely the illustration that two energies – consciousness and creative energy – are needed to create the manifestation. Misunderstanding this point has led many people to wrongly interpret the Tantric tradition and parts of Sivaism (the worship of Siva as pure Being or Purusha). The Tantric tradition has nothing to do with sex in itself, even though some branches of ritual can embrace sexual union, as well as other much less pleasant endeavors! The basic point of the Tantric tradition as a whole is that everything is divine, everything is pure consciousness or Purusha, therefore nothing should be rejected or shunned. Additionally, the tradition uses the propagation of the divine feminine principle, Prakriti or Sakti, to reach Purusha pure consciousness. As we shall see this is the basic principle of the Samkhya. Tantra then is actually the worship of the Divine Mother in either Her fierce or friendly form (left or right hand paths). Yet the purpose is to go beyond any form by merging into the formless.

Prakriti, like Purusha, has three main attributes or qualities that form the basis of all creation. In Sanskrit they are called the three *Gunas* or *Mahagunas*. Guna can be translated as attribute, or quality, literally it means to bind or hold together. Hence, everything that is in the creation has a mix of these three attributes. Their names are *Sattva*, *Rajas*, and *Tamas*, or purity, action and inertia. They are described as follows:

Guna	Cosmic Qualities	Mental Qualities	In Creation
Sattva	Purity, light, clarity, flexibility, harmony, virtue, luminous	Creativity, flexibility compassion, open, kindness, loving, caring, intelligent, humanitarian	Development
Rajas	Active, dispersing, movement, dynamic, force, abrupt, impulse, distraction, turbulence	Direct, aggressive, motivated, goal seeking, angry, controlling	Dispersing
Tamas	Inertia, darkness, obscurity, rigid, fixed, dull, heavy, solid, obstructing, matter	Delusion, dullness, stupidity, deceiving, manipulating, dishonest, depression	Degeneration

The Gunas are often misunderstood and classified as being 'good or bad'. This is missing completely their role in creation. Tamas, the quality of darkness and decay is what allows new growth and creation. It allows life to end, the night to come and for us to fall asleep at night. Actually the entire physical universe comes from the Tamas principle of Prakriti as it represents the more solid, dense aspect of creation and eventually the five elements.

At this time it is important to interject a new concept that is important throughout the study of Samkhya or any of the ancient disciplines. The universe is multidimensional. Trying to give a fixed meaning to any of the principles will result in a misunderstanding because the meanings change according to the dimension being spoken of or experienced. This is a key point of effectively using Samkhya as a tool of transformation in Yoga. This is also the most commonly misunderstood point I find when teaching others.

As we proceed through the steps of creation – through the Samkhya – we can call each of these steps a 'dimension'. Purusha is the most fundamental dimension – that of conscious intelligence. Prakriti then follows as the fundamental principle of creation or manifestation as represented by potential matter. Each additional step after these represents another dimension of the creation. Hence, looking at any of the attributes, or gunas, changes enormously depending on the dimension they are viewed at.

For example let's use the illustration of Tamas, the attribute of darkness, obscurity, and inertia. On the cosmic level matter derives itself from Tamas, on the level of the cosmic mind tamas manifests as obscurity of Purusha, a veiling effect of the source of the cosmic mind. On the level of the individual mind Tamas presents itself as the idea of separation through veiling the cosmic mind (Mahat) instead of Purusha. Tamas becomes responsible for form as the manifestation begins to take shape in matter. The inertia allows the matter to solidify out of gaseous, heated forms. In the human body it allows for sleep and rest. In the human mind it caused delusion, depression, perversion, violence and addiction.

Therefore, looking at any attribute (guna) of the manifestation without first defining what dimension is being addressed will lead to misunderstanding and a wrong interpretation. *This is perhaps the most important point in understanding the Samkhya explanation of creation.*

The three primary attributes of manifestation are responsible for exhibiting all forms of the universe. At each level of the creation we will have to observe their causal influence. The universe takes form through the influence and direction of these three attributes of Prakriti. Nothing can exist without them in either individual or combined forces (pure or mixed forms of matter). They can also be seen as three forms of the creative energy, Sakti, each one representing an aspect of Her divine force.

As we have seen so far Prakriti, latent matter, exists as a potential. In and of itself it is not materialized, it is the potential of matter. That potential exists in three primary attributes, also latent. Prakriti comes into being through the subtle movement of Purusha, pure consciousness. Purusha is the conscious intelligent principle of the universe which, when combined with latent matter, begins the process of manifestation through the three attributes (triguna) of Prakriti. The three qualities of Purusha, Satcitanand, are present in all aspects of the creation and in all three of the attributes of Prakriti.

"One should know that Prakriti is surely Māyā and that the great Purusha is the ruler of Māyā. This whole universe is truly pervaded by the appearance of creation." Shetashvatara Upanishad, 4.10

The Concept of Dualism vs. Monism

The Samkhya usually describes the union of Purusha

and Prakriti as the beginning of dualism and the state of Purusha alone as being monism, or oneness. When these subtleties are experienced rather than learned intellectually another understanding is reveled.

The religions of the world can be divided into either monistic or dualistic approaches to the divine. Monistic represents the concept that there is 'one' and everything comes out of that principle. This is why scholars declare that Purusha, the pure consciousness that is unknowable, is representative of monistic approach. Additionally, when Purusha unites with Prakriti, latent matter as pure energy, the principle of two is born. With two experiences can occur, when there is one alone experience cannot happen.

In fact, both Purusha and Prakriti are in the dualistic dynamic. Existentially this can be experienced. Therefore, Purusha has to be the latent side, the dormant side of the dualistic principle. Furthermore, it can be given three qualities, Satcitanand, through which it can be known. The experience of "One" is before all possible concepts, however subtle. Hence, the only way that one can truly be in Monism is through being the 'substratum'. That experience is final, it finishes all other concepts.

The Principle of Prana

As soon as Purusha, pure consciousness, arises there is, as an integral part, the principle of Prana. Prana is the purest form of energy. It arrives in the beginning and follows each and every step of the creation. It can be seen on every dimension and allows for the whole creation to manifest (See the Brhadāranyaka Upanishad, 1.iii.1-28 for the role of prana in the creation and self-realization, and the Prashna Upanishad).

With Purusha prana can be called the 'energy of Being', the 'energy of Consciousness' and the 'energy of Bliss' (*satsakti*, *citsakti*, and *anandsakti*). With Prakriti prana can be simply called 'Sakti', or the energy of creation through other less common names are used. The interesting thing about the pranic principle is that it is rarely spoken of in the Samkhya, but is a given, an integral part of the system. Without a clear comprehension of the role of pure energy the Samkhya will be misunderstood. The Prana cannot be known directly, but can be experienced as energy without any attribute – its purest form being the 'energy of Beingness'.

"Like the spokes on the hub of a wheel, all creation is fixed on Prāna - Riks, Yajus, Sāmas (the Vedic mantras), sacrifices, Ksatriya and Brāhmana." Prashna Upanishad II.6

5
THE MANIFESTATION / DOWNWARD MOVEMENT OF CONSCIOUSNESS

"Since the Absolute is subtler than the subtlest, It is devoid of names. It is beyond the senses, the mind and the intellect. It is the ever luminous Lord of the creation." 2.10

The interrelationship of the two primary cosmic principles begins the process of creation. Metaphorically the Samkhya describes this as the downward movement of consciousness. The movement of creation is from non-manifest purity (i.e., Purusha and Prakriti) to subtle matter and then to solid matter. The creation is given the metaphor of a downward movement due to the nature of matter's tendency to descend until it solidifies. An example of this is when moisture exists in a subtle form, carried by the wind and atmosphere, until it gathers together in the form of clouds. When the clouds gather enough mass the moisture 'falls' in a downward motion to the earth in the form of rain.

Mahat – The Cosmic Mind
The union of pure consciousness with pure creative

energy gives birth to universal mind or *Mahat*. This next level or dimension of the creation manifests the cosmic principle of intelligence. Every future dimension or level of creation must have the principle of intelligence because Mahat symbolizes this quality of nature.

While the Purusha represents pure, un-manifested consciousness, Mahat represents that consciousness manifested as intelligence. Through the process of manifestation this cosmic intelligence is no longer observed as 'pure'. This is one of the primary differences between Mahat and Purusha. Yet Mahat, as the first cosmic principle, is present in all creation and is omnipotent, or all pervading.

Prakriti, Nature as pure energy, gives its quality of existing to Mahat. Without Prakriti the cosmic mind would not be able to manifest because it is Prakriti that gives form to all things. Additionally, the three attributes of Prakriti begin to take form in Mahat. Therefore, if Mahat contains the three attributes of Prakriti it must also contain the three qualities of Purusha. Mahat is actually born from the three Gunas (attributes) of Prakriti, specifically rajas the attribute of action and creation though movement.

One of the most interesting aspects of Mahat is that it can be confused with either Prakriti or Purusha on account of it containing the three attributes of both. There are a number of ways this can happen. Many people at one time or another have the sense of cosmic well-being or merging with the universe. This brings an incredible peace and serenity to the individual. The sense of the universality of creation is very strong and the individuality is lost for the duration of the experience. This is Mahat, the Being, Consciousness, Bliss of the cosmic mind. The other attributes of nature, Purity, Action, and Destruction can also be experienced at this level, either through deities or directly. *If it is possible to experience, then it is in the dimension of Mahat* – as both Purusha and Prakriti cannot be experienced in any way.

It is at this level that the concept of a universal god or deities manifests. They are an outcome of the cosmic mind and cosmic intelligence. In certain dimensions they can manifest as beings of light and pure thought. All deities belong to the dimension of Mahat according to Samkhya. In order to make Prakriti accessible to the individual minds of the creation, i.e., humans, animals, etc., Mahat takes on subtle form. In the Hindu tradition this is when the trinity of Brahma, Siva and Vishnu manifest.

This is not meant in any way to offend worshipers of these deities, but rather to show that these deities are one cosmic energy whose purpose is to dissolve back into the prior state. Prakriti is forced to take on a subtle form of the deity in order to entice the devotee into merging into herself. When this happens through worshiping the form of the deity eventually merges back into its source, Prakriti, then Purusha. Hence, all deities are forms of the cosmic mind – that intelligence which wishes to lead us back to the non-manifested purity of Being, Consciousness, Bliss.

Mahat is also the inherent intelligence of Mother Nature. It is Mahat that is the driving force of universal intelligence - the intelligence that causes the planets to turn, the flowers to grow, and the seasons to change. Everything in the manifestation is under the control of this cosmic intelligence. This is why the deities can control the manifestation because they are not other than a different aspect of this same cosmic mind.

At this stage of the development of creation there is no concept of the individual. Up until this state there is only the sense of oneness, of unity. This is why the Hindu gods are often quoted as saying they are not other than a 'rival' god. For example Siva is quoted as deferring to Vishnu or one of his forms and saying that Vishnu is omnipotent. Then in another scripture Vishnu will be quoted as saying the same thing – that Siva is, in fact, the source of all creation. This can be confusing to the human mind which operates only from the concept of individual differences. In fact, these deities exist as one cosmic principle – they are not separate from each other – they only appear like that to beings created later – which are why they can say in all honesty that they are not different than the other deity.

The Prana, pure energy, manifests in the dimension of Mahat as the energy of intelligence. In this dimension it takes on the purity of Sattva, pure universal intelligence. In Mahat Prana also takes on the active principle of Rajas and causes the rest of the creation to be formed through its movement. And lastly Prana united with Tamas allows the cosmic mind to take subtle forms.

It is worth noting that modern conceptual thinking does not recognize that Nature, in and of itself, is intelligent. The material approach of modern science, which is usually limited to the narrow concept of 'building blocks', however small, can never penetrate the process of creation until the basic level of universal intelligence is recognized and honored.

Ahamkara – The Sense of 'I'

After the dimension of cosmic mind the creation begins to divide itself into separate manifestations. The beginning of this process is the *Ahamkara* or sense of 'I'. This refers to the development of the individualized concept. Everything following the Ahamkara in creation has a sense of being separate from its source. On one hand this sense causes great anguish and suffering. On the other hand it causes the diversification that makes the world rich in both name and form (*Nama – Rupa*).

The anguish and suffering come from the sense of being separated from the cosmic mind, the joy of being in communion with Satcitanand, or Being, Consciousness, Bliss – the manifestation of Purusha through Prakriti and Mahat. All human suffering can be traced to this diversification, to this change in dimensions. Yet, this same diversification allows for the infinite variety in nature and its manifestation. By this process of separation from the cosmic mind the creation become infinitely rich and full.

The Ahamkara is that dimension when the individual comes into being. It is often translated as 'ego'. This description is deceptive and not entirely correct. Ahamkara has little to do with the Freudian concept of ego because it is far larger in conception. However, it is correct to say that the concept of Ahamkara includes the notion of the Freudian ego. The Ahamkara represents all diversification in the creation where the ego of Freud is concerned only with the individual conceptualization of the human being. Ahamkara is concerned with the whole universe and the basic principle of separateness.

The Ahamkara is also not the same as the Freudian ego even where the individual human is concerned. The Sanskrit word Ahamkara can be translated as 'that which fabricates the 'I'. *Aham* means 'I' and *Kara* is a verb which means 'to make'. So Ahamkara is an ongoing activity, it is being created constantly, every moment. The Upanishads often call the Ahamkara 'the I thought' (The Aitareya Upanishad gives a good summary of the creation and how the mind covers Purusha). These definitions refer to a development before the ego. They refer to the basic sense of beingness that is the foundation of the mind and all its mental and psychological functions. According to Samkhya the Ahamkara or 'I' is the foundation of the whole psychology. The sense of 'I' or separation needs to be there before the ego can exist. It is the foundation of who we think we are; our identity.

When the psychological functions subside or cease (as in the cessation of thought), then the sense of 'I' is very noticeable. In this experience it becomes obvious that the 'I' thought is the foundation of the entire mental existence. Due to the existential nature of the Ahamkara it cannot be understood through reasoning – it too can only be experienced as the most common fundamental component of individual diversified nature. Every person has the sense that they exist and state 'I slept badly' or 'I slept well' or 'I dreamed last night'. It is the Ahamkara who knows, even in deep sleep, what has happened because it is the substratum of the personality dimension.

When the ancient texts speak of the Ahamkara dimension for a human being they usually use the term "*Jiva*" or "*Jivatman*". The word Jiva is often translated as 'soul'. However, the 'I' thought is a better definition for Jiva than soul and lacks the Christian connotations. So when we speak of the Ahamkara on an individual level it means the same thing as Jiva - the individual consciousness as separate from the cosmic mind (Mahat).

In the Ahamkara Prana manifests as the energy which both divides the individual from the cosmic mind and also the force/energy that maintains its separateness. The Prana in this dimension can be seen as the power that holds the 'I' thought (Jiva) in manifestation. It is like a form of glue that holds the Ahamkara in the manifestation. At the same time it allows for the complete diversification of the universe through the energy of movement which is its primary quality. On this level the Prana acts like a chain to bind the Jivatman (individualized consciousness or soul) to the Ahamkara. When Prana stops this action the Jiva leaves the body and the incarnation ends.

Buddhi – The Individual Intellect

The Buddhi arrives in the manifestation with the diversification of Ahamkara. The moment an individual human exists the potential of Buddhi is manifest. Buddhi, or intellect, does not exist in other forms of life. It is the Buddhi, or reasoning mind, which separates the human being from the animal kingdom. However, according to the Samkhya the intellect only exists as a potential – each individual has to develop it themselves. Otherwise the intellect remains dormant.

This then gives enormous freedom to the process of creation – the freedom to remain as a two-legged animal or

The Samkhya View of Creation

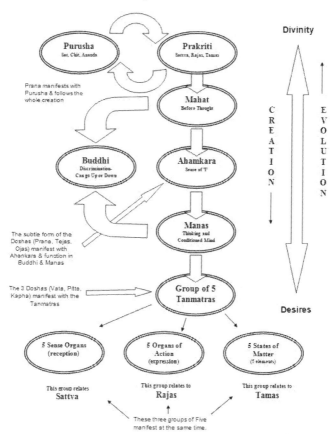

to become a human being. This is determined by the use of the Buddhi – the reasoning mind. If the primary factor separating humans from animals is a faculty that is left unused then how can that being be called truly human? The Samkhya is not a fatalistic system – nature provides for full freedom on all levels of the creation, this is most apparent in the level of human potential.

The Buddhi actually comes directly from the Mahat – the cosmic mind. It is our own little piece of the cosmic or divine mind. It is the highest quality given to the human beings. However, it cannot manifest without the presence of Ahamkara, the sense of being an individual. Only through the diversification of the universal into the individual can a dimension be opened for Buddhi to exist. The name 'Buddhi' comes from the same Sanskrit root as 'Buddha' – from *bud* meaning 'to know'.

Prana manifests through Buddhi as the power of discrimination. This is the power to distinguish truth from falsehood, the Ahamkara from Mahat. When the Prana is low or deranged then discrimination is lacking in the individual. On a lower level the Prana manifests as energy of reasoning. This is the middle level of the Buddhi – the level of philosophy.

The Buddhi is usually translated as 'intellect' or intellectual function. Attention should be brought to the fact that 'Buddhi' is much greater in scope that these concepts allow. The Buddhi can perhaps be better understood through looking at the three levels it functions on. On its highest level it is the power of conscious discrimination, which is feeling, caring and sensitive. On this level of functioning the Buddhi is not dry, nor analytical. It is piercing like a fire *(Tejas)* and is also warm like fire on a feeling, humanitarian level. This is the domain of Sattva (purity) in the Buddhi. This is the aspect of Buddhi that dominates in a developed human being according to Samkhya.

The second level of Buddhi is the Rajasic (active)

level. This relates to the logical, reasoning, dry critical aspect of Buddhi. This is the domain of modern science and is the part of Buddhi that is worshipped by modern society. However, it is insensitive to nature and life due to its dominance of Rajasic, dispersing energy. The lowest level of the Buddhi relates to the dogmatic, fixed intellect that holds on to any rigid, fixed intellectual concept. The following chart gives an overview of Buddhi.

Levels of Buddhi

Level	Guna (Attribute)	Relation to Intellect
Higher	Sattva	Discriminating, humanitarian, feeling
Middle	Rajas	Logical, critical, reasoning, scientific
Lower	Tamas	Dogmatic, fixed, rigid concepts

Manas – The Individual Mind

After the concept of the individual, Ahamkara, the universe is in multiplicity. This gives rise to the 'Mind', or *Manas*. In this sense the word 'Mind' refers to several levels of function. Manas, or Mind, is not just thinking and is certainly not reasoning which is the middle domain of Buddhi. Manas is comparable to our whole psychology. It is more of a field, a thing, than an abstraction. The Mind, or Manas, has form and can be observed – thus it can be treated as an object. *This is a primary part of understanding the Psychology of Transformation in Yoga.* The treatment of the mind as an object in the Vedic / Yogic tradition provides the possibility to transform the psychology as it is an observable object.

The mental functioning can be divided into four clear levels to be better understood – 1) unconscious (or subconscious including the collective unconscious) and memory; 2) feeling mind, thinking mind and emotional mind, also the conditioned part of the mind; 3) individuality, sense of 'I', the part of the mind that relates to time; and 4) the reasoning mind which is Buddhi. The following chart helps to visualize this view.

In Sanskrit these four levels are called: *Chitta*, *Manas*, *Ahamkara* and *Buddhi*. In other words Chitta is the basic level of mind which includes the unconscious and collective unconscious minds of humanity. It propels us to seek mates, reproduce to maintain the species, and find food. It is the level of the mind common with the animal kingdom and includes instincts. Life memories are stored here as received and experienced by the second level of mind (Manas).

Samkhya Levels of the Mind

Level	Sanskrit Name	Function
1	*Chitta*	Unconscious (or subconscious including the collective unconscious) and memory.
2	*Manas*	Feeling, thinking and emotional mind, also the conditioned mind.
3	*Ahamkara*	Individuality, sense of I, part of mind that relates to time.
4	*Buddhi*	Discriminating, reasoning, logical, conceptual mind, intellect.

Manas is the feeling, thinking, emotional mind and also that part of the mind which is conditioned by family, friends, city, country and race. Manas is the part of the mind that modern psychology is primarily concerned with. It is the part we are the most aware of in our own minds. It is also the most unstable as it is influenced directly by the senses and outer environment. *It is the part of the psychology that receives outside impressions and brings them into the mind* – this is why it can be conditioned. It is also common to the animal kingdom.

Ahamkara is as described above with the additional factor of time. Prior to the Ahamkara the concept of time and space does not exist. With the differentiation from cosmic intelligence (Mahat) both time and space come into being. So not only does Ahamkara have the quality of individuality - of 'I' - it also gives birth to time and space. Therefore, the primal memory is stored in Ahamkara as the 'I thought' or the primal thought of individuality, but not memories of our life. Thus when the human body dies the memories of individual experiences that are stored in Chitta disappear. Time and space also disappear with the death of the mind. The Jiva (soul) remains eternal, but without any individual mental memories. The Jiva stays bound to the memory of 'I' by the Prana and is held in subtle space and time waiting for the next incarnation.

Lastly, the Buddhi represents the intellectual part of the mind as described above. In ancient scriptures like the Upanishads these four parts of the mental functioning are called collectively 'Manas'. However, in the Samkhya, Manas refers specifically to the emotional, thinking and conditioned mind. Secondarily, Manas refers to Chitta, or unconscious mind. According then to Samkhya the Manas and Chitta aspects of the mind are lower in manifestation than the Buddhi and Ahamkara.

Manas refers to our psychology, or emotional mind, our feelings and how we are conditioned by life. This level of individual mind is basically the same in animals as humans. This can easily be observed through pets that one can condition and who are definitely able to feel and have emotions themselves. Their psychology may be more primitive, but it follows the same basic principle as for humans. The level of Chitta, or unconscious mind, is the same for humans as for animals, but tends to change somewhat according to species.

Manas is our daily thinking mind. It allows us to function on a 'normal' level and relates to both our environment and other people. If the Manas is disturbed or traumatized in some manner then the other aspects of the mind suffer in both function and interrelationship.

Manas is our individual door to reality because it is an organ of *both reception and expression.*

Prana manifests on this dimension as the power to think or the movement of thought. Aggravated Prana will disturb the mind and cause excessive movement of thought or it will cause cloudy, obscured thinking. Having Manas in harmony means that the Prana is stable and moving easily. If the Prana is low then the thinking process is marred and psychological problems can result.

On this level the three attributes of Prakriti (latent matter) becomes important to the human being. Manas is properly the realm of purity or Sattva. If the other two (Rajas or Tamas) begin to dominate the field of Manas then mental disturbances arise. The level of Chitta or unconscious mind, is the realm of Tamas as it is hidden, deep and obscured from normal life. The Ahamkara is the level of Rajas, action and energy, because it divides the Cosmic Mind into the individual mind and cosmic multiplicity. This force of movement and action is behind all of human behavior. Buddhi is also the domain of Sattva, but like Manas can be affected by both Tamas and Rajas.

"The mind (Manas) is superior to the senses; the intellect (Buddhi) is superior to the mind; Mahat is superior to the intellect; Prakriti is superior to Mahat. Superior to Prakriti is the Purusha who is all pervasive and is without worldly attributes, knowing Purusha a man becomes free and attains immortality." Katha Upanishad, 2.3.7-8

Tanmatras – Matter in Subtle Form

Until this moment the universe has remained in a subtle, divers state. The principle of differentiation has come into being (Ahamkara) along with the ability to perceive it (Manas). Now, the next dimension of the universe arrives as a five-fold division of subtle matter. The universe is still without solid form at this point. One can say that 'name' or classification has arisen with the mind, but not yet 'form' in a subtle or solid sense. With this five-fold division of matter subtle form comes into existence.

The ancient scriptures often speak of 'name and form' arising with the sense of the individual or Ahamkara. This is absolutely correct, however, one should differentiate that the form is still subtle as in the functioning of the mind. This is why Manas is called a 'thing', or object, because it exists in form. Solid form has not yet been able to manifest because there has not been enough direction given. With this new dimension of matter as subtle form solid matter has the potential to manifest.

In Sanskrit the word *Tanmatra* can be translated as 'primal measure' or 'root action'. It is the cause of all solid matter as we know it. The Tanmatras are potentials of matter – they themselves are not matter – they are the potential of matter. They are directly responsible for the five main divisions of matter, or categories of matter. At this point in the creation the Prana divides itself five-fold as well. It can be argued that the Tanmatras are primarily the division of Prana as it becomes more dense or solid. Hence, the Tanmatras are a dynamic force that are driven by the five divisions of Prana (*prana, udana, vyana, samana, apana*).

The Tanmatras represent the five states of matter in a pure form. The scriptures describe these states of matter as – a field or space, movement of gases, transformation, liquid or cohesion and lastly, solid. All of the manifested universe can be put into one of these five categories. The Tanmatras represent these five states of matter in their purest form. In order for matter to come into being there needs to be an interaction between these different states – the dimension of the Tanmatras is before this interaction.

The Tanmatras (or five-fold subtle division of Prana) also have the unique ability to power the senses of biological life. The Tanmatras are the energy that allows the object to be perceived by the senses of reception (sense organs). They are actually the exchange of energy between an object and the one perceiving the object. Without their presence no object can exist, but neither can it be perceived. One way of understanding these powers is to see them as dynamic energies that both cause form and allow it to be seen.

Still another way to understand the Tanmatras is the through the Vedantic idea presented in the Upanishads. They state that there is present in all duality a subtle trinity. This trinity manifests on different levels and under different names, but can be seen or observed at all times. First, there is a perceiver, then an object to be perceived, and lastly the action of perceiving the object. The perceiver is the Ahamkara using the organ of Manas; the object is the material or subtle form made from the five States of Matter; and the action of perceiving is the Tanmatras (all of the ten major Upanishads refer in some way to this trinity – observer, object of observation, action of observing; seer, seen, action of seeing; this concept of the trinity is central to Vedic and Yogic thought and can also be used as past, present and future).

The level of the Tanmatras is also the level of the dream, astral or subtle worlds. The heavens and other non-physical dimensions all exist here in this level. The Tanmatras are the cause of the astral universe and control all functions there. However, note that the mind (Manas) is before the astral plane and controls it, as it is the source of the Tanmatras. Therefore, the mind (Manas) has the power to create a whole subtle universes; any world, or plane that can be conceived in the mind can manifest due to the Tanmatras.

The Five States of Matter

On this dimension form comes into being. Prior to this level nothing has existed in a concrete, stable, solid manner. The five states of matter come into being because of the previous dimension – they cannot exist without it. The ancient texts give the following analogy to the *Pancha Maha Bhutani* (five primary states of matter) to help the student comprehend their formation and function. "From the void of nothingness there arose a subtle movement of consciousness. As this movement became more concentrated various gaseous substances manifested. The movement of these gases caused friction, which began to transform the gases into humid condensation. This condensation began to solidify and create liquid as a cohesive substance. Finally, this liquid settled and solidified into solid matter."

The texts further state that 1/10 of space becomes gaseous, and 1/10 of gas becomes transformative heat, and 1/10 of heat becomes cohesive liquid, and 1/10 of liquid becomes solid. Therefore, solid matter contains a small part of each of the others. This is the interaction of matter that allow for manifestation to occur. Only space, or ether, remains pure and each of the other states has some portion of the previous states.

These states interact causing all matter to manifest from this interaction. These states of matter represent categories – all matter can fit into one of these five categories. Unfortunately, they are usually translated as the 'Five Elements', which gives a very erroneous idea of what they represent. The word 'element' has little to do with the alive, interactive state of matter that is meant by the Sanskrit word *Bhutani*.

State of Matter	Attribute	Element
Field	Space	Ether
Gaseous	Movement	Wind (Air)
Transformative	Heat	Fire
Humidity	Cohesion	Water
Density	Solid	Earth

These five states also manifest ideas and concepts – they are not limited to physical form, but also influence subtle form through the Tanmatras. This dimension is the dimension of alchemy and other ancient sciences like astrology and Yoga. This is dimension where the five forms of Prana create worlds based on mental concepts or ideas. Whatever we believe will tend to manifest here, for better or worse as the case may be.

State of Matter	Conceptual Ideas
Field	Connection, communication
Gaseous	Movement, direction, velocity
Transformative	Transformation, light, perception
Humidity	Cohesion, unity, holding
Density	Solidity, stability

The five states of matter are the basis of all ancient sciences. They are the result of direct observation and can be experienced in life and observed directly. They are existential, experiential and experimental in nature. The whole universe is comprised of these categories and comes into existence through their interaction. They are profound and require contemplation to comprehend, as they are also metaphoric for the various archetypes of nature as a whole.

The Five Forms of Reception

Once matter comes into existence there needs to be some means to perceive it. The ancients observed that the five forms of matter were received respectively by five sense organs. These five forms of reception receive the name and form (classification and structure) of the five principle categories of manifestation.

They are often called the five 'sense organs' in the ancient texts of Samkhya and the Upanishads. Yet, the Sanskrit word is far more potent in depth and meaning. *Jnanendriyani*, means something closer to 'the *potential* to receive, on all levels, experiences of the physical, mental and subtle world'. These five forms of reception are mainly concerned with how the psychology receives impressions and information from outside. All impressions that are taken in are received by Manas.

These functions are the same for animals and humans. Actually, the three groups of five, "five states of matter", "five forms of reception" and the "five forms of expression" all come into existence together. All three comprise the physical universe that is common to all forms of life on earth. The plant and mineral kingdom lack both the five forms of reception and expression, yet do contain the five Tanmatras on the astral or subtle world.

On this dimension the Prana manifests as a binding and communicating power. For the five states of matter the Prana manifests as a binding power which allows the states to interact and combine. It holds them together or apart as needed. On a biological level, as in Ayurveda, the prana is often called the *Tridosha* Theory (or Vata, Pitta, Kapha). On the level of reception it is the prana that allows the movement from the object to the sense organ and the coordination of the senses themselves. On the level of expression it is the prana that allows the movement of expression and even the ability to express.

The Five Forms of Expression

Just as there is a need for the reception of the manifestation so too there is a need for the interaction with this universe through expression. Hence, there is a counterpart of expression that correspond to the five forms of reception. Ultimately, the Upanishads state that Pure Consciousness, Purusha, manifests in order to interact with itself. This is sometimes called the divine play or 'Lila'. Therefore, the means of both reception and expression are necessary for the Purusha to experience itself (the Mundaka Upanishad has interesting insights on this subject).

Without some means to express the circle of creation is not complete. There has to be a way to express either the joy or pain of the impressions received in the manifestation. This allows the freedom to respond according to the attribute, or Guna, that is predominating in the mental dimension. If the attributes are of a pure nature (Sattva) then the expressions will be creative, beautiful and harmonious to the situation. If the attributes dominate in the psychology are extroverted (Rajas) then the expressions will be dynamic, aggressive, and goal orientated. If the attribute that is dominating the mind is languid (Tamas) then the force of inertia prevails through expression of negative emotions and even the lack of expression itself.

Tables of Relationships

State of Matter	Reception	Expression
Space – Ether	Sound – Ears	Speech – Mouth
Movement – Wind	Touch – Skin	Grip or Hold – Hands
Heat – Fire	Sight – Eyes	Motion – Feet
Liquid – Water	Taste – Tongue	Emission – Urine-Genital
Solid – Earth	Smell – Nose	Elimination – Anus

On one hand the very act of expression is the end of the creation. Thus, it can be both the end and beginning of the creative process. When the attributes of harmony and peace are prevailing in the mental dimension then this cycle becomes productive and supportive for all of humanity. When the other attributes prevail then the expression is destructive for the creation and humanity as a whole.

The Twenty Attributes of Nature

In order to recognize which state of manifestation is present there is a logical system of identification in the Samkhya. This system is related to the dualistic nature of manifestation and represents the 'masculine/feminine' or 'negative/positive' aspects of polarity in creation. They exist in ten pairs and all objects or states can be placed in one of these pairs. It is not an extensive list as other pairs can be found, but these are regarded as the most primary and important when understanding the qualities of creation.

Negative / Cool	Sanskrit	Positive / Hot	Sanskrit
Cold	*Shita*	Hot	*Ushna*
Wet	*Snigdha*	Dry	*Ruksha*
Heavy	*Guru*	Light	*Laghu*
Gross	*Sthula*	Subtle	*Sukshma*
Dense	*Sandra*	Flowing	*Shara*
Static	*Sthira*	Mobile	*Chala*
Dull	*Manda*	Sharp	*Tikshna*
Soft	*Mridu*	Hard	*Kathina*
Smooth	*Slakahna*	Rough	*Khara*
Cloudy	*Picchila*	Clear	*Vishada*

These twenty qualities are subdivisions of the three Maha Gunas (attributes) of Prakriti; Sattva, Rajas and Tamas. From the interrelationship of these three primal attributes arise the ten pairs of opposites, *Gurvadi Gunas*, or Twenty Gunas. Hence, they are directly related to Prakriti, latent matter. They are used specifically to classify matter on all levels. In astrology they are used on a subtle level to understand archetype energies of the planets, signs and houses. In Yoga they can be used to understand both asanas and pranayama – in application and therapeutic result. In Ayurveda they are used to understand the five states of matter and their controlling dosha. They are also used equally in diagnosis and treatment.

The following table shows how the twenty attributes or Gurvadi Gunas relate to their source – the three Maha Gunas (attributes) of Prakriti (matter).

Guna	Qualities
Sattva	Neither cold nor hot, neither wet, nor dry, light, subtle, mobile, soft, smooth, clear
Rajas	Hot, little wet, little heavy, gross, flowing, mobile, sharp, hard, rough, cloudy
Tamas	Cold, wet, heavy, gross, solid, static, dull, hard, rough, cloudy

All matter can be classified by using these ten pairs of opposites. This classification provides the methodology to use the Samkhya as a base for medicine, astrology, psychology or any physical science. They exist in all objects and situations of life. They can always be observed and used to understand the creation. They provide a working model of the subtle and observable universe. Through them we can understand the natural balance of nature that works through opposite forces to maintain equilibrium in the creation according to the Vedic perspective as seen by the *Rishis* or sages.

6
THE RIGHT AND WRONG USE OF THE MANIFESTATION

"The Absolute is neither male nor female nor neuter. It is not a matter of perception or reasoning. Why do you wonder over whether the Absolute is blissful or devoid of bliss?" 1.47

The downward movement of Purusha, Pure Consciousness, causes the creation to manifest through Prakriti. The upward movement of Purusha from matter is called Self-realization or 'moving toward Self-realization'. This is because the 'self', or essence, of all life forms is Purusha. Hence, realizing one's 'self' simply means know that Pure Consciousness (Purusha) is the source of all creation. This is applicable for individual humans and also on a general level. Hence, the manifestation as a whole has the possibility to move upwards towards Purusha, as do individual humans. Self-realization is also called enlightenment and exists before time or space - hence it is not a process.

As mentioned in the two previous chapters there is not any real purpose behind the creative manifestation of matter. However, the ancient texts do declare that two important concepts manifest during creation:

1) If consciousness wishes to experience itself it needs the Jiva in manifestation

2) Once manifestation is experienced it is possible for the Jiva to reunite with Purusha while remaining in a physical form

The second is the most important aspect of the Samkhya for the modern person seeking transformation in their life because it offers an alternative to the prevailing mental material continuum.

According to Samkhya this is the basic purpose of life – first to experience life and then to reunite with the source of life, Pure Consciousness. Any other use of the creation – according to Samkhya – is a waste, or at the very least, a misuse of the incarnation.

A number of different points arise with this view. One primary question is why Purusha manifests the creation at all, if the purpose is only to return to itself? The ancient texts give us the answer that there is a tremendous respect for freedom. If there were no manifestation there would also not be a choice to return to the source of the creation. Hence, the Samkhya is a life positive, non-fatalistic approach to the creation on all levels (the Bhagavad Gita addresses this in detail, as does the Shvetashvatara Upanishad).

"Purusha and Jiva are both birthless - one is all-knowing, omnipresent and one is ignorant and limited. Prakriti (Māyā) manifests the enjoyer, enjoyment and the object of enjoyment. The Self is infinite as it is the source of the universe - it is not the cause and has no attributes. One becomes liberated when one knows this trinity to be nothing other than Self." Shvetāshvatara Upanishad, I.9

We must understand the right uses of the manifestation itself if we are to use Samkhya as a practical system to bring transformation, health, happiness and peace to others and ourselves. This obviously begins with understanding how things come into being and in what order that happens. This was explained in the last chapter.

The key to using the creation in a beneficial way revolves around the Buddhi, or intellect. The Buddhi has the ability to move upwards or downwards in creation. As it comes directly from the cosmic mind (Mahat) it can easily move upward into a non-fragmented state. Buddhi also has a special relationship with the conditioned mind, or Manas. When Buddhi is controlled by the conditioned, emotional mind there is a general downward movement into desires and material existence.

Manas, the conditioned, emotional mind, is a great servant and lousy master. When Buddhi, the intellect, is in an upward movement then Manas is a good servant. However, when Manas dominates the Buddhi then it becomes the master and drives the individual to a downward non-evaluative movement.

Manas, our psychology, relates to the creation through the Five Forms of Reception (sense organs) and the Five Forms of Expression (organs of action). Thus the key to regulating the mental and emotional functions is through the right use of the senses (reception). Wrong use of the senses will cause Buddhi to come under the sway of Manas and led to desire and entrapment. This is because Manas gains more power than the Buddhi when the senses are over used, or when used in a destructive manner.

A simple example of this can be seen from a patient of mine who has high blood pressure. I gave her a list of foods that are known to increase blood pressure and told her to avoid them altogether if possible. Unfortunately, her emotional mind was stronger than her intellect and she continued to eat chocolate, drink coffee and wine, all of which increase blood pressure. She chose to take a chemical pill rather than to develop good habits that her intellect knew were right. Emotionally she needed the 'feel good' foods like chocolate and coffee which were slowly destroying her metabolism. Even though her Buddhi knows what is right, her conditioned mind (Manas) will not permit Buddhi to take action.

In the Samkhya system the emotional mind creates and maintains desires. Excessive use of the senses and Manas causes excessive desires. It can be stated like this – desires are manufactured by the conditioned, emotional mind; received through the five forms of reception; and gratified through the five forms of expression.

For example, I walk down the street and see a chocolate cake. My emotions go, "Hum, that would sure taste good!". My intellect goes, "I'm not hungry, I just ate lunch". Which of these will win? Will the intellect decide or will the emotional mind decide?

In the above example health is the primary concern. Obviously eating a chocolate cake once in a while is not going to harm the body. However, if the emotional mind is very strong then people can take an excessive amount of a 'nutrient negative' substance (e.g. chocolate cake) which will ultimately ruin their own health. Health is not the only level on which this works. This same scenario applies to psychological habits as well.

When the gratification of the senses becomes the primary focus in life then the creation is wasted. This means when food, sex, money and sleep become the primary goals of an individual then they are no longer moving upward. According to Samkhya these goals are the same goals that motivate animals – food, sex, comfort, sleep. I have exchanged comfort for money because money is what, in modern times, buys comfort. Consequently the ancient texts say that this kind of life is the same as an animal – therefore a wasted human birth.

The right use of the manifestation is to have and enjoy food, sex, comfort and sleep – but not as the primary goal or direction of life. There is nothing wrong in having pleasure. The problem only comes when pleasure or sense gratification becomes the dominating current in the mind. This then becomes the main objective of life. Keeping the primary objective focused on humanitarian goals is one way to profit from the life on this planet. Another is to orient yourself to finding the source of the creation or the source of the 'I' concept. This last is the highest goal of humanity according to Samkhya.

My teacher used to say that mankind as a whole was only interested in food, sex and sleep. He would say many times that it is rare to find someone who is interested in discovering where they have come from. Finding out where we have come from also gives the knowledge of where the entire creation has come from. *The Samkhya is the direct observation of people who have discovered their own source.*

The key to this knowledge is the right use of the intellect or Buddhi. As explained in the previous chapter Buddhi exists only as a potential in humans. It has to be developed and used. Additionally, it is not the dry kind of intellect we associate with the word 'intellect'. Buddhi is the reasoning and analytical power of the mind – but has a compassionate, loving side to it.

The Western use of intellect implies reasoning without love or compassion. Quite the contrary is the case with the Samkhya sense of Buddhi. The definition of Buddhi's highest quality is discrimination. With a developed Buddhi one can differentiate between the real and non-real (Pure Consciousness and Manifestation). This power of discrimination is also the power of love. *Truth is love and being able to discriminate between love and non-love is the highest quality of Buddhi.*

One cannot differentiate unless there is some experience of the two components involved. Buddhi contains the loving aspect of Mahat, the cosmic mind, because consciousness intelligence is love itself. Mahat manifests the qualities of bliss, joy and peace. It would be impossible that the child of Mahat, Buddhi, would not have these qualities as Samkhya clearly states that Buddhi is the individual piece of Mahat in human beings.

What we call 'intellect' in modern culture is only the middle level of Buddhi. The archetypes of the University professor who has an over developed brain and memory is not a person who has a developed Buddhi according to Samkhya. When Buddhi is developed as a whole it presents a well-rounded human being, not a neurotic 'intellectual' or the brilliant 'absent minded professor'. These kinds of individuals often have great gifts of intelligence, but this is not the higher state of Buddhi.

Buddhi chooses truth, beauty, and harmony on all levels of life through its power of discrimination. Buddhi includes love, compassion and kindness that may be lacking in the modern definition of 'intellect'. The Buddha or Christ show a developed Buddhi that has the capacity to lead one upwards to the cosmic mind and eventually to Pure Consciousness itself.

This then is the correct use of the creation according to the Samkhya system. When the majority of people are unhappy and dissatisfied in modern culture it can be both empowering and enlightening to consider the Samkhya point of view – not only of creation – but to use this creation itself for the betterment of ourselves and humanity.

"When the organ of intellect continually associates with an uncontrolled mind, it becomes devoid of discrimination and the mind behaves like the unruly horses of a war chariot." Katha Upanishad 1.3.5

Karma

Another aspect of an overly strong Manas and weak Buddhi is that of karma, or the law of cause and effect. Karma itself is a much misunderstood term. Its literal translation from Sanskrit is 'action'. It is very simply the law of cause and effect, nothing more or less. Thus each action results in a response or effect. There is no such thing as 'good or bad' karma. There is, however, a very clear understanding that 'effects' are directly related to 'causes'.

This means that certain kinds of behavior will 'breed' the same kind of results. The misunderstanding of 'good and bad' comes from this direct relationship between cause and effect. Humanitarian actions tend to bring humanitarian results and so on. The problem with understanding karma arises because of our obsession with the material conceptual universe. Culturally we view everything according to a material basis. Samkhya, however, is concerned with the manifestation of consciousness and the self-awareness of this consciousness in manifestation.

Because of this difference of orientation confusion arises. Karma is not limited to one physical incarnation in the manifestation. Karma is linked directly to the individual consciousness by the prana. The prana binds the Jiva (soul) to the Ahamkara, the manifestation and the karma. Therefore, 'good' actions may not be visible or may not manifest in the lifetime where the 'cause' happened. The karma is bound to the Jiva (soul) and is given different names in Sanskrit – *Vasanas* or *Samskaras*. These translate as latent impressions that are stored and carried into future incarnations. Hence, as long as the Jiva exists then karma will be bound to it by the prana.

The basic concern of creation after the manifestation of matter is the union of the individual Jiva with the universal Purusha. Karma plays an important role in this return, as it is the primary preventative factor or obstacle. Hence, the teaching of Samkhya and the Upanishads is that one should not create karma in the first place – either 'good or bad' – because both are binding the Jiva to the creation. It is important to understand how karma is created and then how not to create it (the Bhagavad Gita is the clearest text on the subject of Karma).

It is through the Ahamkara that karma is first possible

and second comes into being. This is the key point in manifestation. However, it is really the functioning of Manas (conditioned, emotional mind) that creates karma. The Ahamkara needs an 'organ' in which to 'cause' things with and Manas is the 'organ' of the 'I' or Ahamkara. Just as the five sense organs allow the Manas to receive information so Manas is the organ of reception for the Ahamkara; likewise with the organs of expression and action.

Manas is then the vehicle for Ahamkara to function in the universe. Specifically it is through the actions of Manas that karma is created. The regulating factor in this process is the upward moving Buddhi who can help the individual unite with Mahat – effectively bypassing the Ahamkara and the karmic process. If however, Buddhi moves downward then the Manas is given even more power to bind the individual to desires which led to the identification with the actions.

Desires are a causal factor of karma. In other words desires create karma. This is why some of the major world religions give such a nasty place to 'desires'. Nonetheless, this term is also grossly misused and frequently misunderstood. Desires are neither 'good nor bad'. The best way to define 'desires' is in the context of Samkhya and the ancient Vedic disciplines. To do this it is necessary to return to the basis of creation. That basis is the movement – up or down – of consciousness. When the basic orientation of the Ahamkara is downward moving (as manifested through Manas and Buddhi) then there are desires. This means the need to experience the manifestation through the senses and the identification as the 'I' who is acting out the experiencing. When, however, the basic orientation of the Ahamkara (again through Manas and Buddhi) is upward moving then karma slowly ceases to be created because the Jiva begins to identify with Mahat instead of the 'I' or experiencer.

Another way of saying this can be as follows. When we

identify as being individuals karma is manufactured. When we identify as Mahat the cosmic principle of Purusha, karma is not produced. Karma ceases altogether when the identification of the individual is lost into Purusha. Even in Mahat there is still a subtle cosmic level of cause and effect going on.

The stronger the Manas is the more karma will be produced. If Buddhi moves downward due to the Tamas Guna then the karma becomes even stronger. The right uses of the senses (or expression and reception) are extremely important in that they help to create more or less karma. One should note however, that according to Samkhya a thought alone creates karma because it is an active 'thing'. Remember that the mind is considered to be an object. Therefore, a thought will have to have an effect or result as it is an object of the mind.

The whole question of karma comes down to what you hold in your mind (Manas). On a secondary level it depends on what you express. If death and destruction is your expression it must also be in your mind. The same applies for desires. There is actually a beautiful story about desire.

"A prostitute and priest lived in the same neighborhood and would often see each other when they passed in the street. As time passed the prostitute eventually died and shortly after her death the priest also passed away. The priest came to the gates of heaven and was surprised to find out that he was going to be sent to hell. In shock he happened to look through the gates and see the prostitute waving back to him from heaven. Outraged he asked why, when he had spent his whole life in the service of the Lord, he was not allowed into heaven. But the prostitute, who had spent her whole life in service of earthly pleasures, was allowed in heaven. The angel replied, 'during the execution of her profession the prostitute was only thinking of our Lord, while you, on the other hand were only thinking of the prostitute'".

Desires are like this – they reveal the depths of Manas, the conditioned mind. Our actions are of secondary importance when karma is concerned. In the case of the above parable the lifetime actions of the priest were not strong enough to change the karma created by his mind, or the lifetime desire of lust. Hence, it is possible to say that thoughts are karma, or that karma is the result of what we think.

The right use of the manifestation according to Samkhya, and the ancient disciplines that are based on it, is to strive for union with Purusha. The science of this process was called Yoga, from the Sanskrit root 'yug', literally 'to join'. In modern society yoga has been reduced to a physical practice of postures. The system of Samkhya itself is Yoga, a practical methodology of reuniting the individual to the primal cause of creation.

Samkhya considers any other use of the manifestation a waste. Note that love is a short cut to primal Consciousness and the path of devotion, or Bhakti, does not really come under the domain of experiential Samkhya. My teacher has said several times that it is very difficult for Westerners to follow this path as the principle of Ahamkara is so strongly developed through Western conditioning. Women find this way easier than men. Yet, regardless of which method, path, or system one employs the emphasis is on merging into the original source of creation, Pure Consciousness or Purusha.

7
LIBERATION / THE UPWARD MOVEMENT

"The creation of the subtle and gross universe is neither for you nor for me. The shameless mind created the idea of diversity. There is neither unity nor diversity for you or for me. I am Existence-Knowledge-Bliss (satchitanand) and endless like space." 3.39

According to the classical texts of Samkhya the Purusha, or Pure Consciousness, never loses its quality of unity during the process of creation. Even when the principle of individuality arises with the dimension of Ahamkara Purusha remains pure and intact. Hence, Samkhya is based on unity, not on fragmentation. According to this view all life is one basic unit and even through diversification it still remains as one conscious principle.

When teaching Samkhya as part of other ancient disciplines I am often asked about other life forms and where they fit into the creative process. The Samkhya that has been illustrated in the previous chapters is primarily describing the creation of matter as a whole and its relationship to conscious intelligence. This is the basic evolutionary scheme of different life forms after the five states of matter manifest. As one can see from the chart there are different degrees of evolution within the animal, plant and mineral kingdoms. This information is general and can be divided further into more specific categories if needed.

Top of Creation	General Species Group
	Humans
	Mammals
	Birds
	Reptiles
	Fish
	Insects
	Shell Fish
	Trees
	Flowering Plants
	Lichens and Moss
	Amoebas or Virus
	Crystalline Minerals
Bottom of Creation	Non-Crystalline Minerals

At the end of the creative process we have seen solid matter manifested as non-crystalline minerals, or rocks and stones. Purusha is also present at this level and still maintains its purity and wholeness as the causal factor of creation.

The Samkhya explains that all creation has the potential to return to the primal state of Purusha. What is clearly stated in the texts is that all of the manifestation will eventually return to its source Purusha. This can roughly be described as conscious evolution.

Evolution in the context of Samkhya is different than modern concepts. From the ancient point of view the physical body of form is just a vehicle for the individual consciousness, or Jiva, to return to itself – the primal Purusha. Emphasis on the physical form is negligible. The focus is on the Purusha, first its diversification and later its reintegration. In modern science the emphasis is only on form as exemplified by Darwin and later by modern physical sciences.

There are many names and terms to try and describe the apparent division of Purusha in creation. This point has been debated for many thousands of years and can never be known by the intellect or reasoning. Both the ancient Upanishads and my teacher are emphatic that Purusha remains as it is throughout the process of creation – it remains as the undivided primal beginning. This baffles the logical mind which cannot understand that something can be divided and yet remain unchanged.

Perhaps one way to understand this is to relate it to a field in which everything takes place. Even though there are activities in the field the field itself remains unchanged. The 'field' of Purusha is both before time and space, name and form. It is the cause of these, not the outcome of them. As the cause it is before and maintaining the apparent reality of these divisions of time and space. As our minds function in both time and space it is impossible to truly understand the capacity for Purusha to be both 'oneness' and multiple simultaneously.

Once these contradictions are either experienced, accepted or understood it is possible to proceed in the comprehension of evolution as expounded by the Samkhya system. Evolution refers to the Jiva, not the form or species. Evolution is concerned with the reintegration of Jiva with the Purusha. Furthermore, the Jiva has never been separate from Purusha – so in the sense of modern thought there is no evolution – only a return, a homecoming. Instead of 'evolution' an 'upward movement' is used to describe the return of Jiva to Purusha. There is no evolving process in this return so it cannot correctly be called evolution.

This is the 'open secret' of the mystics from all religions. This is the true purpose of humanity – to realize that they already are both the source and the outcome of creation. Realizing and living this truth has been called by different names, enlightenment, realization, Christ consciousness, freedom or liberation.

In this upward movement of Jiva to Purusha many forms are used. The most ancient texts say that there are 40,000 different species that the Jiva moves through. The last of these species is the human being. My teacher used to say that this process takes 35 million years to arrive at a human birth. This is why the Samkhya declares that the purpose of human birth is to discover that Jiva and Purusha are the same and prevail in all beings. Failing to perceive this reality causes a downward movement in creation. Hence, a failure to know reality causes the Jiva to incarnate in a less evolved form.

The evolution of species is nothing other than the movement of the Jiva on its return to Purusha. This is the doctrine of reincarnation. The movement of Jiva through different species is nothing more than the incarnation, again and again, of Purusha coming home to Purusha. According to Samkhya there is no real species evolution – there is adaptation – but not the transformation of one species into another one. According to Samkhya each species represents a dimension of creation that Purusha can experience something. The movement through different species happens so that Purusha can experience different occurrences as part of creation. This was the "non-reason" for the creation in the first place – for Purusha to experience itself.

According to Samkhya the incarnation of Jiva in human form is a peak moment in the slow return through 40,000 different forms of life. But one human birth is rarely enough. The movement through human births is also long and can take many thousands of incarnations to achieve the final insight that everything is Purusha. Thus we have humans who behave like humans, those that behave like animals and the majority someplace in-between. The values and goals of the individual show the placement of the human birth.

Ultimately every Jiva that seemingly divides itself from Purusha will return to Purusha. This is the purpose of the creation. The overall flow of the conscious creation is 'upward', that is its purpose according to the Samkhya system. This means that everyone will eventually merge back into their original nature of undivided Purusha. This will happen because it is a natural part of manifestation.

In this process free will is paramount. Without a conscious decision on the part of an individual an upward movement toward Purusha is not possible. Personal choice is a fundamental condition of Samkhya. Without consciously choosing to become more conscious an individual has the total freedom to descend into the senses and pleasures that give birth to endless desires. Choosing to stop the creation of desires is perhaps the most difficult, yet important change a human being can make.

Several thousand years ago there developed a school of thought that described everything as 'illusion' or *Maya*. One main aspect of this teaching is that desires are unending and will keep the individual in a downward movement. Hence, this school gave the name 'Maya', or illusion, to Prakriti – latent matter. This is because all desires can be traced back to the primal level of latent matter. All of the creation arises from this Prakriti including desires. Therefore, the founder of this school declared that all creation was an illusion because it manifests as name and form, time and space, as dual in nature. Desires reinforce this process of creation.

Stopping the downward movement of desires into more creation can happen to anyone at any time. The Samkhya is vague on this point – what makes an individual choose the upward movement of consciousness? My teacher had two different responses to this question. One was that it was luck or merit, meaning there was no direct reason. The other answer – which was very rare and less common – was that a person needed to have a predominance of the Sattva Guna (attribute of harmony and peace) in the psychology.

Tragically this point is not well understood in modern times. The understanding of the Upanishads is that a person needs to have an ego before they can go beyond it. In this way the human potential movement that began in California in the 1960's helped many people prepare for the eventual reintegration of Jiva to Purusha. *However, many people wrongly assumed that this process of reintegration was a substitute for psychotherapy or psychiatry.*

One needs to be healthy in mind (if not body) to be able to develop the Sattva attribute in the Buddhi, its vehicle. Carrying emotional damage prevents Sattva from developing and delays the homecoming of Jiva to Purusha. My personal observation in both India and the West is that emotionally or mentally damaged people that pursue "spiritual" practices think they are harmonious, peaceful and pure in nature (Sattva). This form of self-delusion shows a lack of Buddhi and its highest trait of discrimination. Self-examination is, without doubt, the most valuable tool a human can develop.

Without discrimination the mental function will stay in various states of delusion and imagination. Human beings need to be healthy mentally in order to return to the source of consciousness. The Samkhya says that the Manas, or conditioned mind, is the most sensitive organ of the human. If this organ of reception is damaged then it is very hard to repair. Examples of this can be seen from war survivors – like Vietnam veterans. Children in particular are susceptible to being damaged in the emotional, conditioned mind.

Modern studies are beginning to show that children who are war survivors remain traumatized their whole life. I personally know people who are now in their eighties who grew up in Europe during World War II. These people watched, as children, adults and children being killed in front of their eyes. They grew up with bombs dropping around their houses at night. One woman I know still has nightmares at the age of eighty and continually grinds her teeth and moans at night.

Choosing the upward movement of creation is humanity's ultimate goal. However, take time to put the psychology in order and resolve past issues. Otherwise the individual remains emotionally immature or unable to relate to the material society that most people perceive as 'normal'. This can be seen from people teaching meditation or yoga for twenty years and who have disruptive personal relationships, or who manipulate their students in the guise of 'knowledge' or as 'gurus'. Furthermore, some individuals believe that repeating sound syllables several minutes a day is sufficient for both personal and spiritual development. Even though sound does have an important function in the creation, alone it will not bring spiritual fulfillment. Chanting mantras (sound syllables) will not resolve emotional problems or a disturbed psychology. It does work on harmonizing the conditioned mind (Manas), which is of value and can aid psychotherapy.

While the above view may not be popular with many people involved in teaching Eastern methods it is my observation over the last forty years. My own teacher expressed a similar view after experiencing a number of very psychologically disturbed people coming to him in India for spiritual fulfillment. His comment was that these people are so damaged from a lack of love in their childhood that transformation and re-integration is virtually impossible. People who are damaged though a disturbed family life should first make an effort to become healthy psychologically before pursuing the subtleties of this method. If this is not done there is a risk of simply advancing any authoritative person as a parental substitute, mother or father, as the case may be.

The beauty of Samkhya is that it is experiential. The

difficulty with using the Samkhya as an experiential method is that one must be healthy mentally and have a good sense of self-worth. Otherwise the Buddhi cannot function in its highest capacity of discrimination. If these aspects of Samkhya are understood then there is great potential for conscious 'evolution', or reintegration with Purusha.

What then is the methodology of Samkhya? Actually there are several main ways to use the Samkhya existentially. There is not one way for all people. Three main approaches can be examined. The first is using the Buddhi or mind to help perceive reality through the development of Sattva. The second is to use the prana or energy of Purusha through breath. All methods come out of these two primary paths. All meditations can be divided between these two approaches. The way of love or devotion – the original teaching of Christ, Krishna and other religious teachers – is separate from the two others.

The path of devotion (Bhakti) does not use the Samkhya directly although it can be understood with Samkhya. Love is a kind of short cut that heals all psychological wounds and bypasses other forms of practice. This path of devotion is very effective to bring the devotee to Mahat or even Prakriti if really lived existentially. Unfortunately, people tend to think that devotion is easier, when in fact, it is perhaps the most difficult. But eventually all of these three methods have to disappear with Prakriti and the dual creation. Actually, all creation has to disappear on its own before Purusha can be lived instead of being intellectualized. This can only really happen by directly questioning where the 'I' thought (Ahamkara) arises from and living the answer existentially.

8
THE YOGIC METHOD OF
TRANSFORMATION

"Because the Absolute is subtle, invisible, and without qualities, the eight limbs of yoga have been prescribed by the yogis to realize It, they should be followed, one after the other." 2.15

By far the most common ancient science in the Western world is Yoga. For the majority of people Yoga means Hatha Yoga and primarily the physical postures associated with its practice. The physical side of Yoga is important as a foundation to health and to help purify the physical and subtle bodies. This in turn has an indirect effect on the mind.

Yoga is classically called Ashtanga Yoga – or "the eight limbed path of union". Of these eight branches only one or two are commonly practiced in the Western world. In the West we practice asana and occasionally pranayama. Unfortunately we miss the basis of these two which are Yama and Niyama. Equally a problem is the misconception of the eight terms of Yoga – especially of Yama and Niyama. Once more it is only though the Samkhya system that we have the correct context to understand Yoga as Yoga is based on Samkhya. The eight classical branches are:

1.	Yama	Inner purification (awareness of conditioning)
2.	Niyama	Outer purification (awareness of actions)
3.	Asana	Physical purification (awareness of body)
4.	Pranayama	Subtle purification (awareness of breath)
5.	Pratyahara	Moving Manas inwards (Pancha Jnanendriyani or five senses)
6.	Dharana	Focusing Buddhi inwards and away from Manas
7.	Dhyana	State of being (meditation)
8.	Samadhi	Identification with Purusha

It is best to re-define the eight branches of Yoga according to the vision of the Vedic seers as illustrated by the Samkhya system. The first term *Yama* includes five categories and provides the person with five methods of inner purification. The function of these five inner purification's is to become aware of our psychological conditioning. Conditioned mind is Manas and so these five methods are primarily concerned with the function of Manas. Once we become aware of our conditioning we become free of it which stops the downward movement of the Ahamkara through Manas and five senses and motor organs.

The five categories of Yama are:
1. Ahimsa   (non-violent thoughts)
2. Satya   (honest self-examination)
3. Brahmacharya   (awareness of sexual energy)
4. Astya   (desire for objects)
5. Anabhinivesha   (identification with objects)

Ahimsa is usually translated as non-violence. It actually means to become aware of our violent thoughts and how we aggress other people emotionally. According to Samkhya all physical violence comes from Manas or the mind. Hence, becoming aware of our own frustrations and pain eliminates the violent thoughts that tend to manifest outwardly as aggression to others – either psychologically or physically.

Satya is usually translated as truthfulness. It actually means to be honest in self-examination. Without self-examination we cannot become aware of how our Manas is conditioned. A lack of honesty in this process causes complete failure in the purification of the mind. We can only start from where we are – a failure to recognize honestly where we are stops all possibility for the Jiva to return to Mahat and so Purusha. Hence, truthfulness is an inner process that in turn slowly manifests as truth in recognizing Purusha in all things.

Brahmacharya is usually translated as control of sexual energy. It actually means to abide in Brahma (another name for Purusha). Unfortunately, humans tend to behave more like monkeys because they think that by imitating a saint – who is no longer interested in sexual intercourse – they will become like the saint. Brahmacharya in the context of Yama means developing awareness of sexual energy. Sexual energy is the energy of life and the suppression of it cuts one off from life itself. Likewise excessive indulging in sexual activity disperses life energy and causes the mind and body to become weak, thus reinforcing the downward movement of the Ahamkara. Becoming aware that the most fundamental desire of humans to be loved and needed is the root thought behind sexual desire. All sexual activity begins with a thought and so awareness of the root desires prevents indulgence. The development of awareness also liberates more energy to other activities that may have gone into sexual relations alone. At the same time abstinence from sexual pleasure is harmful and causes the mind to become obsessed with sexual thoughts. It is a joyful and pleasant activity that brings health to mind and body when the root desires and thoughts are discovered through awareness.

Asteya is usually translated as not stealing from others. It actually means not to desire objects, or the desire for material possessions. This does not mean that material objects are bad or that something is wrong with owning things. It refers to the basic desire of Manas to entangle itself in the material manifestation by becoming obsessed with objects. In the extreme this means stealing things from other people. Yet, the real meaning is our mental relationship with the material world. Once again there is nothing wrong in it unless our mind and psychology become obsessed with objects and things. Consequently, looking at our conditioning objectively and seeing if our main priorities in life are materialistic, humanitarian or spiritual in nature is a basic step of self-development and transformation in Yoga.

Anabhinivesha is usually defined as non-attachment or non-clinging to objects or relationships. It actually means the identification we have with thoughts, objects or relationships. Once more it is the function of Manas that is important. If the mind is obsessed with an object or person then the higher functions of Buddhi cannot manifest and the person will be held in the lower realms of the creation. This is often misunderstood that one should not be in couples or in relationships. In fact, a marriage can be the best way to help develop the Buddhi and Sattva in a person. Hence, our tendency to 'own' or identify ourselves with objects and people is what prevents the upward movement of Manas and the development of Buddhi. Non-attachment means not to be attached to mental concepts – the strongest of which is 'I am body'.

The second step in the eight-fold approach of yoga is *Niyama*. It includes five categories and provides the person with five methods of outer purification. The function of these five outer purification's is to become aware of our physical and mental actions. While the Yama's are concerned with our inner mental functions the five Niyama's are concerned with how we manifest them outwardly and so are also concerned with Manas.

The five categories of Niyama are:

1. Santosha (acceptance of what is)
2. Shaucha (act without personal gain)
3. Sadhyaya (study of scriptures)
4. Tapas (focused behavior)
5. Iswara Pranidana (identification with Mahat)

Santosha is usually translated as contentment. It is the total acceptance of what IS at any moment. This acceptance brings outer contentment because we do not carry an idea of what should be happening.

Shaucha is usually translated as purity of action. The term means to act without personal gain and so stop the creation of karma. The only pure action is one that is not creating karma. Hence, to act without the idea of personal benefit or gain is purity of action.

Sadhyaya is usually translated as self-study. It is the action of focusing the person on the upward movement of creation. This means the search for an association with truth. Truth or consciousness is mainly found through scriptures and writings of the seers. Although this can also mean to live with a teacher and absorb truth through his or her presence and verbal teachings. The individual needs to make a physical effort to stop the downward tendency of the mind and creation.

Tapas is usually translated as austerities or discipline. It means to become determined to seek the source of creation or consciousness. Bringing this desire to the front of Manas is what is meant by Tapas. Having other desires than becoming one with Purusha is not Tapas.

Iswara Pranidana is usually translated as surrender to

god. Iswara is the personalized god that manifests with Mahat. Pure consciousness manifests in an image so that Manas can comprehend the unknown, un-manifest. This can mean any surrender to the divine – with or without form. It is very difficult to pass directly to the formless so surrender to the Guru or a God is more accessible for most people. Surrender can also simply mean love – it does not imply 'giving one's self up'. As in love, surrender means to lose the concept that you exist as Ahamkara instead of Mahat – cosmic consciousness. In other words there is a re-identification from the individual to the cosmic consciousness or Mahat.

The third branch of Ashtanga Yoga, *Asana*, is the most known and practiced in the West. It is concerned with physical purification and developing awareness of body. There is little need to explain the purpose of physical exercise and the benefit it has on physical health. However, asana is much misunderstood in the West as simply a means to exercise the body when in fact it is a means to develop awareness of the body though movement. Asana practice that leave out this aspect cannot really be called Yoga or be a part of the ancient Indian tradition. It works mainly on the five elements or the body, but also has an effect on the Tanmatras or energetic levels of creation through the five forms of prana, or pancha vayus.

The fourth branch of Yoga is called *Pranayama*. Unfortunately, it is usually translated as control of breath, or breath control. Actually Pranayama means to develop the awareness of breath. This results in a subtle purification of both the physical body (five elements) and the Tanmatras (subtle body). These in turn both affect Manas and allow the mind to turn upwards. Pranayama is strongly purifying to the energetic body. Controlling the breath usually gives good health, but re-enforces the downward movement of Manas into the physical universe. Overall the modern tendency of Yoga teachers and practitioners is to control the body, breath (energy) and mind. Unhappily, this actually increases the downward movement of the Ahamkara and Manas through strengthening the sense of the 'doer' or 'I'. However, it does bring good health and a strong ego. Perhaps this is why several of the most famous Yoga teachers alive today are known to have strong egos and occasionally violent tempers.

The fifth branch of Yoga is called *Pratyahara*. This is usually translated as control of the senses. Like its predecessor Pratyahara is also not really concerned with control, but rather awareness of how we use the five senses. Pratyahara is actually concerned with moving Manas in an inward direction. Or, if you like, to reverse the movement of Manas so that Buddhi can begin to function. The natural movement of Manas is outward through the five senses (*Pancha Jnanendriyani*) and it requires some conscious attention to stop this tendency and allow Buddhi to receive the prana that is normally moving out through the senses. This is perhaps one of the most important steps in Yoga and is also perhaps the least understood. The methods of turning Manas inwards can be physical, but true Pratyahara is simply the mind not moving outward because the desires are no longer there to pull it outwards. For the beginner using methods to stop the five senses can be useful but quickly give the erroneous idea that the senses are the goal and not Manas itself which is the filter and receptacle of the sensory impressions.

The five branches mentioned above are the supports or foundations for the last three branches of Yoga. They are sometimes called the 'outer supports' or 'outer aids'. The five of them function together and should be used together. Using one of these alone will not result in a change of Manas and its identification with Ahamkara. Meaning that it will not develop into a union with the divine or Yoga. Thus, the use of asana alone is worthless from the perspective of Samkhya.

Dharana is the sixth branch of Yoga. It is a method of focusing the Buddhi inwards and away from Manas. Only at this point can one begin to work directly with Buddhi. Prior to this all work has been with Manas, Tanmatras and the three groups of five that make up the solid universe. Dharana is often called concentration. This could be correct if one is aware of the difference between Manas and Buddhi. Otherwise it just is a method to increase the strength of Manas the conditioned mind. Real Dharana is concerned with developing the highest aspect of Buddhi, which is discrimination. Without discrimination the last two steps of Yoga cannot be achieved or even attempted. Unless Dharana is developed by right use of Manas meditation is impossible, as is the re-identification of the individual with the cosmic. This is because the definition of discrimination in Samkhya is that which never changes is real and that which changes is unreal. This prepares the ground for the next branch.

Dhyana is often called meditation today. Actually what modern people do is more the sixth step of Dharana. Dhyana, the seventh branch of Yoga, is a state of being that has resulted from the previous six branches of Yoga. It is an effortless expression of Buddhi returning back to the Mahat. In this case there is still the Ahamkara (individual) who is aware of being the cosmic intelligence. However, at this point the Ahamkara is greatly weakened and try's to manifest the Buddhi's return to Mahat as an experience. If the Ahamkara succeeds then the state becomes an experience and Buddhi returns to its normal role as a servant to the Ahamkara. On the other hand if the Yoga continues then the state of being develops into the eighth branch.

Samadhi is the last branch of Yoga where there ceases to be an individual to experience Mahat, the cosmic consciousness. When this happens the Jiva is absorbed into Prakriti where several last pitfalls await to trap the person into remaining the experiencer of the bliss of unity with un-manifested matter. Samadhi is often a temporary state with most yogis and they have periods of absorption and non-absorption. These are the subtle traps of the latent matter and three Gunas of Prakriti. This also corresponds to the sheath of bliss (anandamaya kosha) in the Yogic anatomy of Self-realization. True Samadhi is permanent and is the natural outcome of avoiding the traps of temporary Samadhis. Once the Samadhi is permanent then the yogi is not different than Purusha, or Sat, Chit, Ananada. Beyond this there is simply 'Turiyatita' (beyond the fourth state) which some people call 'Parabrahman' or the Substratum.

Thus Yoga can be seen in its correct context of the Samkhya as a practical tool to return to the Purusha, or pure consciousness. This is indeed the purpose of the Yoga Sutras of Patanjali who came long after the Vedic period, yet who based his sutras on the Vedic approach of creation and consciousness. This is for a very fundamental reason: it is the experience of every enlightened sage though each expresses it in a slightly different manner.

Vaidya Atreya Smith

9
VEDIC ASTROLOGY AS A METHOD OF TRANSFORMATION

"In the Absolute, time and its divisions, such as morning and evening, have all been denied. The primordial elements, such as fire and air, have also been negated. But the Ultimate Reality cannot be denied, being this same Absolute, O mind, why do you weep?" 5.24

One of the most popular systems from ancient India is Vedanga Jyotish, Vedic or Indian astrology. It is gaining popularity extremely fast in Western countries due to the strong predictive powers contained in this system. This system is strongly based on the mathematical analysis of astronomy. Jyotish, or the 'science of light', is the science of time as seen through both astronomy and astrology. Unlike other forms of astrology it is based on astronomy and works with the actual position of planets in the sky.

The danger of using any system of prediction is that of misinterpretation. Misunderstanding can easily happen because of the multidimensional nature of the universe – of which the birth chart is a reflection. There is a grave need for a methodology that explains the multidimensional nature of the universe. Without this structure the practitioner is more likely than not to misinterpret the chart through a narrow one or two dimensional approach. Hence, using Vedic astrology without a good comprehension of Samkhya is fundamentally wrong and self-deceiving.

Unfortunately, many people only read charts on one or two dimensions – usually material and psychological. For example the moon can represent, the mind as a whole, the intelligence, happiness, beauty, emotions, our conditioning, the feminine principle, women in general, the mother, and the cosmic mother - Prakriti. Being able to look at each dimension individually is extremely valuable and important. Without the structure of Samkhya these different levels of the creation can become confused and intermingled – leading to confused readings and wrong interpretations.

Table 1. Relations of Planets to Samkhya

Planet	Cosmic Dimension (Primary)	Cosmic Dimension (Archetype)
Sun	Purusha / Prāna	Agni (God of Fire)
Moon	Prakriti / Matter	Varuna (God of Water)
Mars	Prana	Siva
Mercury	Buddhi	Vishnu
Jupiter	Mahat (positive)	Indra
Venus	Five Tanmatras (astral planes)	Devi
Saturn	Mahat (negative)	Brahma
Rahu	Manas (it obscures the Moon)	The Human Masses
Ketu	Manas (it obscures the Sun)	The Human Individual
Ascendant	Ahamkara	Separation / Karma

The most fundamental level of the birth chart applies to the cosmic overview that Samkhya gives. The chart itself represents the total manifestation that has arisen out of Prakriti or Latent Matter. So on the ultimate level the birth chart is the manifestation and the space supporting the chart (i.e., room, office etc.) is the Purusha. It is important to remember that the chart is representing duality and is in duality. Therefore, it is not really possible to read the chart beyond the prime component of duality – Prakriti.

On the level of cosmic creation (Prakriti) we have primary and secondary relations. There are several ways to view these relations and some people may not agree with the following reasoning. The chart above outlines possible relationships on a cosmic level, but is not fixed; other interpretations can exist.

Starting with the Sun we can see that it represents first the Purusha as undivided pure consciousness and then the divine archetype of Agni (god of fire, transformation) on the level of Mahat. Sun as the main energy of the universe also represents the cosmic prana, especially the Chitsakti or the energy of consciousness. The Moon can be seen as Prakriti as it reflects the light of Purusha (Sun) and then as the divine archetype of Varuna (the god of water, cohesion).

Mars is the planet of pure energy or Prana and then is represented by the divine archetype of Siva (god of destruction and renewal in this correlation). Mercury can be seen as the power of discrimination in Buddhi and second as the divine archetype of Vishnu (god of preservation and communication in this correlation).

Jupiter is the positive side of the Cosmic Mind, (Mahat) the cosmic intelligence of the universe and second as the divine archetype of Vedic Indra (god of heaven and giver of knowledge). Venus is primarily concerned with the Tanmatras and astral world as it brings us into the five senses and the experience of pleasure. Secondly as the divine archetype of the goddess Devi, wife of Indra. Saturn is the negative side of Mahat and second as the divine archetype of Brahma (god of knowledge in this correlation). Jupiter is the giver of knowledge, Saturn the remover of ignorance, both represent the primal powers of the Cosmic Mind in different aspects.

Both the lunar nodes, Rahu and Ketu, act as Manas in the sense that they obscure the light of the Sun and Moon or Purusha and Prakriti. In this sense the nodes function as malefic energies eclipsing or hiding the light of the divine principles. Additionally, they cause separation from these same principles. Yet, on the secondary level they represent the archetypes of society and the individual as related to the masses. The ascendant represents the Ahamkara in general and the archetype of separation in the universe who also conveys past Karma through its incarnation.

When approaching astrology it is important to keep in mind two factors – 1) the chart represents time generally and the movement through time of an individual (ascendant or Ahamkara); 2) the planets are metaphors for archetypal forces as described in the Samkhya. Hence, the planets are far more than deity archetypes as the Greek system of astrology proposes even though there is a deity relation. The Samkhya system shows the actual forces that manifest the deity archetypal energies present in Western astrology.

Using Jyotish without these basic understandings will lead to confusion, misunderstandings and a general degradation of the system. Vedic astrology can be used to predict very mundane and precise events in a person's life as it is the science of time. The planets by their movement determine night and day as the basic unit of time measurement. (In astrology the Sun and Moon are considered planets even though this is not correct by modern scientific terms.) Using Vedic astrology to determine events is possible without the Samkhya system. This is what most people look for when they approach an astrologer – timings of events or appropriate moments in which to act.

However, the moment the astrologer leaves the domain of time and events it is imperative to understand the Samkhya system. Without it you will look at every Moon as the mother, every Sun as the father, etc. This is a tendency in Western astrology – and with many astrologers who have begun to learn and apply the Indian system. The Samkhya provides the astrologer with a clear scheme of dimensions and levels of archetypes throughout creation.

Illustrations of how this can be useful can be seen from Table 1. In this table we can see the primary and secondary relations of the planets to Samkhya. The Sun, the brightest and most dominant planet (star) in the sky represents the archetype of the Purusha – the primary cause of the creation and pure consciousness. On a secondary level it represents the divine energy of transformation (Agni). When looking at the capacity of an individual to consciously move in the upward direction of liberation or conscious development the Sun is very important.

For example Sun in the 12th house of loss is considered to be bad for self-esteem and projecting oneself in society. It will tend to deny recognition from the public and society in general. However, when seen at the cosmic level of creation the Sun indicates Purusha or the pure Self. In the 12th house it gives strength to Purusha as it is placed in the house of loss – it will remove all indications that are placed in it or the lower indications of the Sun such as ego. For this reason it is a house of liberation or Moksha. As Purusha is the source of all creation everything will be removed leaving only Purusha as the primal force of consciousness.

In Table 2 the Sun is shown on an individual level where it manifests as the Jiva – the individualized aspect of Purusha or soul. On this dimension the Sun in the 12th house again shows an individual interested in losing their personal identity for the greater cosmic identity of Mahat, the Cosmic Mind. Table 3 shows the relations to spiritual study or Sadhana. On this dimension we can see the higher side of Buddhi manifesting as the upward movement to the cosmic mind, Mahat. The Sun in the 12th house will show that the Jiva (soul) is ready to merge into the cosmic level when the rest of the chart supports that movement. If the rest of the chart is non-supportive then it will show that the ego (as in Freudian ego) will prevent that upward movement.

Table 2. Relations of Planets to the Individual

Planet	Higher Individual	Lower Individual
Sun	Jiva (soul)	Ego
Moon	Intelligent aspect of Manas	Emotional aspect of Manas
Mars	Prana – passion for life	Strength
Mercury	Expression	Speech
Jupiter	Knowledge	Material Desires
Venus	Reception / Expression	Sensual Desires
Saturn	Buddhi (discrimination)	Grief and sorrow
Rahu	Manas (collective unconscious)	Chitta Externalized
Ketu	Manas (individual unconscious)	Chitta Internalized

The idea of Sadhana is that a planet can be useful for worldly affaires and worthless or even prevent spiritual evolution. The placement of the Sun is of basic importance as it shows if the person will be able to devote energy to spiritual practice. The Moon will show if there is enough basic intelligence to understand spiritual study. The placement of Mars will indicate if there is enough energy to comprehend study and pursue practices. Mercury will show if there is discrimination to choose the right spiritual study path or teacher. The placement of Jupiter in a chart will show if a teacher will manifest in some form for the seeker. Venus will indicate the possibility of devotion in spiritual practice and Saturn will provide the discipline necessary to follow though in spiritual life. The lunar nodes show the karma we bring and the karma we are likely to create in our pursuit of spiritual life.

Table 3. Relations for Sadhana (Spiritual Study)

Planet	Helpful	Obstructive
Sun	Jiva	Ego / negative will
Moon	Intelligence	Indulgence in Emotions
Mars	Tejas (Fire of Perception)	Dogmatic thinking / Anger
Mercury	Buddhi as Discrimination	Poor logic / hyper thinking
Jupiter	Guru or Teacher	Materiality / indulgence
Venus	Devotion - Bhakti	Senses / sexuality
Saturn	Yogi – discipline	Delay / perversion
Rahu	Externalized	Delusion
Ketu	Internalized	Delusion

The lower or obstructive energy of the planets can also manifest according to their placement and the relations to other planets. For example an exalted Jupiter in Cancer could show that a teacher would manifest through an emotional connection and teach through love, compassion and humanitarian values. On the other hand the same placement could lead an individual to into deep material desires and goals. This would tend to manifest though "acting" as a teacher to others and manipulating people thought emotions and status.

According to Samkhya no planet is benefic unless it lessens the identification of the Jiva with Ahamkara. Thus an exalted Jupiter could be helpful in manifesting a teacher and by giving spiritual inclinations, or it can lead one into the mire of material desires and money. This will depend on the indications of the other planets in the chart and the moment to moment choice of the individual.

An example chart is useful to explore the approach of

transformational psychology according to Jyotish. In the following chart the individual has a difficult birth chart for material affaires and relationships. On the other hand the individual has enormous potential to transform the normal downward movement of Manas. The Moon generally represents Manas in the chart. By looking at the example chart we can see that the Moon is three time afflicted - by its placement in Scorpio; by conjunction with Saturn; and by aspect with Mars.

Me 07:29 Su 07:02 Ve 00:50 Pisces (2)	Ke 27:38 Aries (3)	Ma 08:48 Taurus (4)	Gemini (5)
As 02:31 Aquarius (1)			Cancer (6)
Capricorn (12)			Leo (7)
Sagittarius (11)	Mo 13:46 Sa 21:02 Scorpio (10)	Ra 27:38 Libra (9)	JuR 03:10 Virgo (8)

If one was to look at this chart from a level of personality only one would tend to conclude that the personal relationship of the individual with their mother would be weak and conflictive. That the personality (Manas) would tend to fluctuate between being fiery / aggressiveness and depression. The person could expect little emotional happiness in life and would tend to have to work hard (conjunction with Saturn in the 10th and as lord of the 6th) and have chronic digestive gas (lord of the 6th with an Air or Vata planet). All of these are classic indications of a weak Moon.

However, when we approach the same chart from the transformative view we have a different insight into the individual's potential. Moon in the 8th sign gives depth and transformation to the mind which is helped by the negation of Saturn. As the Yogi Saturn cuts away unneeded concepts and ideas. It gives discipline to the mind and provides strong intuition and perception to the Moon. The aspect of Mars provides pure energy to transform the conditioning of the mind and penetrate deeply into hidden desires. This combination can develop good mental power and discrimination when Ashtanga Yoga (see the previous chapter) is followed. While the polarity of Mars and Saturn is considered highly detrimental for the planet associated with them they also provide the possibility and energy for profound transformation if the individual uses the higher sides of both planets.

The placement of a weak Moon with Saturn in the 10th house would tend to indicate difficulties in professional life and so the potential for change in this area. The Moon is generally good in the 10th house as it helps social contacts and communications; it also represents the public. However, Saturn conjunct the Moon here would tend to remove the social recognition the person would normally receive. On the brighter side Jupiter in the 8th house - a house of Self-realization - that aspects the 12th house - another house of Self-realization would support any movement of the psychology towards inner transformation. This would be especially true if the person met a true teacher. The North Node in the 9th house shows support from past karma towards a spiritual transformation and that much work has been done in this area already in past lives. The present karma is moving towards a house of creativity in the fine arts - it is also a house of ego and individuality (South Node in the 3rd).

This should caution the individual about having material goals as the primary direction of life as it will lead them deeper into identification with the Ahamkara.

One key to this chart is how the person manifests the energy of the second house, an area of family, society, expression and wealth. The grouping of three planets here indicate that the ego may be more concerned with money and social image along with personal relationships (lord of the 7th in the 2nd) than personal transformation. Mercury is too close to the Sun, so Buddhi (Mercury) is burnt and its light cannot illuminate Manas. This reduces discrimination as the highest aspect of Buddhi. While Venus is exalted in Pisces she is also combust with the Sun. The key to transformation in the chart is whether the Sun's archetypal energy manifests as the ego or as the Jiva (soul). As the second house is concerned with expression in society and wealth the Sun in this location may have difficulty to manifest its higher side of the Jiva - and ultimately the Purusha.

Venus could help the Jiva (Sun) through devotion (Bhakti) and strengthen the weak Buddhi. This person should not trust their analytical mind (Mercury as the intellect) as it is combust. However, there is a strong relationship (planetary Yoga) with Jupiter that provides divine grace and power to transform the intellect (Mercury). Hence, through the grace of both Jupiter and Venus the Jiva could turn towards humanitarian or devotional actions that would lead to profound transformation.

This chart would tend to indicate Karma Yoga, or the path of social action, to bring major transformation to the individual. There are many other important indications in this chart including Saturn as the ascendant lord and Atmakaraka (indicates the Soul in this incarnation). The individual has 12 Raja Yogas and planetary debilitation is canceled by several Nicha-Bhanga Raja Yogas which gives enormous power to the person to realize their desires. How the individual decides to approach their life - from a materialistic approach or from a transformative approach - will determine how much peace of mind they have in life.

Decidedly a choice towards money and social position will cause much suffering to the individual with possible periods of clinical depression. However, if the marriage partners do not prevent the natural creativity from manifesting the individual should become very successful and well known in their chosen field later in life. On the other hand the same chart shows ample support for profound personal transformation and happiness in life, mainly through social work and Karma Yoga in which the individual would also become well known. This the freedom of the psychology of transformation in Yoga - the freedom of the Samkhya system. The freedom to suffer through the downward movement of Buddhi or to live in peace and happiness through the upward movement of Buddhi.

A closing note on this chart. Now twelve years have passed since I wrote these original observations. The person has little money, even though having lived quite well for a long period of their life, and struggles daily to pay the mortgage on a house they could not afford; but one that gave the social status they craved. The family relations are strained and the person has since become divorced after a long separation of six years. Overall rather gloomy and not uplifting. The one promising series of events was the return and development of artistic skills. Even though very talented this person was unable to manifest this skill into a concrete activity that they could live from. Unfortunately, the person is mostly obsessed with money and social position so have not pursued any of the higher aspects showing in their chart that would reduce the negative effects manifesting. Free choice is the foundation of the Samkhya – as is the fruit of our actions, Karma.

Vaidya Atreya Smith

10
THE AYURVEDIC METHOD OF TRANSFORMATION

"The Absolute cannot be invoked or abandoned because It is formless. Therefore, what is the use of offering flowers and leaves or practicing meditation and repeating mantra? How can one worship that Supreme Beatitude in which both unity and multiplicity are merged?" 4.1

Ayurveda, like Vedic Astrology and Yoga, is firmly based on Samkhya. Without a good understanding of Samkhya the Ayurvedic doctor or practitioner becomes mechanical in his or her approach to healing. As modern medicine is already addressing healing in this manner there is little need for natural systems like Ayurveda unless they are practiced in a non-mechanical holistic form.

Samkhya gives a different view of the creation. As a model of the universe it is far closer to 'new physics' than Newtonian mechanical physics, because it recognizes a constant field of intelligence. Ayurveda is a holistic system of health precisely because it is not mechanical in approach or practice. It is not based on structure and form as modern medicine is, but rather on systems and function. It is through the understanding of Samkhya that this is possible. Samkhya provides the methodology for this functional approach to the human organism.

Unfortunately, there is a trend in India among doctors to practice Ayurveda in a more mechanical symptomatic manner. Some believe that they are being 'innovative' and modern to treat the disease rather than the person who is manifesting the disease. There is also a firm belief that unless they practice in a more symptomatic manner the patients will not respect them as doctors. There is possibly some truth to this in India, however, in Western countries the trend is exactly opposite. More and more people are looking for alternative approaches to the mechanical structural approach of modern medicine.

Actually this is more than a trend as the media is full of reports that estimate that between 60% of people in the United States and over 70% of Europeans are at some point seeking health care outside of modern allopathic medicine. The main reason given is for 'preventative measures'. Hence, there is a need for an authentic holistic foundation and not another 'natural medicine' based on Mr. Newton's mechanical observations.

The Samkhya can provide this model for any system of medicine; it is not limited to Ayurveda. Although Ayurveda has certain advantages in that it is completely integrated with Samkhya already. In all probability the world medical system of the future will be based on Ayurveda. But also an Ayurveda no longer limited by the many cultural restrictions imposed by the Indian social context.

The real point is to address the human being as an alive organism that is intelligent and naturally strives for a dynamic state of health. According to Samkhya the creation is never in a static state. It is always moving in a downward direction – e.g., more creation; or in an upward direction – e.g., return of consciousness to Purusha. Hence, the definition of health in Ayurveda is that of a 'dynamic' one – one that is *increasing*. In contrast, the mechanical model of the universe does not recognize an intelligent principal in creation nor do they admit that health is something other than an absence of disease.

Samkhya gives Ayurveda the background to define health as 'dynamic'. When addressing the physical human body the downward movement of creation eventually means decay and death. Opposite to this is health or an upward movement of intelligent consciousness. The only real flaw with the Samkhya or Ayurvedic approach to transformation is that one needs a minimum of intelligence to use them. This is, in fact, the crux of the issue.

According to Ayurveda the cause of all disease arises from the concept of individuality or the Ahamkara. The Ahamkara is what separates us from the cosmic mind or Mahat. In Mahat there is no disease (there is also no physical body, which makes matters easier!). The Samkhya perspective is that if the consciousness of a person is identifying itself with Mahat, Prakriti, etc., then health will result. If, however, the consciousness is identifying with the conditioned mind (Manas) and senses then disease will result.

This may seem a bit simplistic or too decisive to the modern mind. However, when examined closely another picture emerges. At the level of the Ahamkara the creation begins to diversify into numerous entities – at this level nonphysical. Additionally, the intellect or Buddhi comes into being. This is our little piece of the Mahat, or cosmic mind. The natural movement of the Ahamkara (individual) is downward into more creation so it can experience itself to a fuller degree. The Buddhi can go either way – up or down.

The downward movement of Buddhi is called *Prajnaparadha* or 'failure of wisdom'. Buddhi then is the key to health because it causes the Ahamkara to move either in an upward or downward direction. Buddhi moving downward is called 'ignorance' or 'failure of wisdom' and upward it is simply called wisdom or intelligence.

This is fairly easy to observe in daily life. Allowing your mind and emotions to move towards the proverbial 'chocolate cake' on a daily basis is ignorance. High daily intake of sugar, denatured food, processed food, chemically treated food, old food (other than fresh), and food with preservatives and colorants are known to contribute to disease. For natural medicine these substances cause disease. Or just smoking a pack of cigarettes a day is enough to show a 'failure' of wisdom. One then would question the intelligence of the modern doctor who smokes IF one uses the Samkhya system. But by using the 'structure and form' approach of modern medicine it is possible to justify the effects of these poor choices for health.

Thus the real problem with Ayurveda and the Samkhya system is not whether it works or not – but whether people want to begin to use their intelligence to choose habits that promote health and consciousness. As stated several times in this book the Samkhya system is a system that respects freedom of choice – including the choice to kill yourself through bad habits.

Occasionally I send clients away without charge when I see that they are unable, or not willing at this time, to take responsibility for their own health. In these cases I suggest they see a 'normal doctor' who will keep the responsibility for their health and poor lifestyle. He or she will then prescribe one or a variety of chemicals that will work on tissue structure rather than the intelligent system as a whole. This approach is effective in preventing symptoms from manifesting that results in the mechanical definition of health – absence of symptoms.

When viewed from the standpoint of Samkhya all disease can be seen as the failure of wisdom. This simply means that our health is in our hands – we have the power to choose habits, foods and lifestyles that promote health rather than reduce it. This can be as simple as putting on a coat before going out into cold weather – a 'failure of wisdom' would be to wear a sweater and later that day catch a cold. There is nothing complicated about this idea, in fact, it used to be called common sense.

Another aspect of the disease process and the Ahamkara is when the prana (intelligent energy of consciousness) fails to maintain its bond to the manifested body. This is one of the primary jobs of the prana on the level of Ahamkara. Before Ahamkara – in Mahat – the prana is the power of cosmic mind and intelligence. It continues with this role in the Ahamkara as the power of intelligence. However, through diversification it also takes on the role of binding the Jiva, individualized Purusha or soul, to the Buddhi, Manas, Tanmatras, Five Senses, Five motor Organs and their vehicle formed out the Five States of Matter – the human body.

Therefore, the link of prana to the Ahamkara is of primary importance. Note that the prana is irrevocably linked to the principle of cosmic intelligence. When teaching I use the example of a piece of paper which, by its very nature, has two sides. For paper to exist it must have two sides. Prana and the intelligent principle are like a piece of paper – each principle is a different facet of the other. Hence, when the intelligence is compromised then the prana becomes weakened. At first this affects the overall vitality of the person and then it slowly begins to weaken the bond with the Ahamkara.

According to Samkhya, when the pranic link becomes weak the Jiva begins to move away from the 'body/mind' manifestation. Death results on the physical dimension. Unfortunately, between health – a strong link of prana to Jiva – and death, there is what we call 'disease'. Usually the categories of disease caused by a weak link of prana to Jiva and Ahamkara are called auto-immune diseases, cancer and most chronic, degenerative diseases. Often this relationship of prana to the Jiva and Ahamkara is called the 'identification of Jiva to Ahamkara'. Still another way to describe it is the Ahamkara's 'self-identification'.

All of these expressions mean the same thing. The Ahamkara – by its nature – identifies with the mind/body in order to manifest. The two key components in this process are the prana (energy of intelligence) and the Jiva (the individual Purusha). One could say with complete justification that Jiva cannot exist without prana as both are derived from Purusha itself. In effect when we say Ahamkara identifies with the body/mind we are saying it bonds to Jiva/Prana. Or when we say that Ahamkara 'self-identifies' it is the Jiva (self) that identifies (prana) as an individual (Ahamkara). Dr. Robert Svoboda expressed this whole process clearly in 1989 in his classic book, *Prakriti: Your Ayurvedic Constitution.* In it he says:

"Without Yukti, the adept combination of attitude and activity to harmonize the individual, indigestion becomes chronic, and mutates into new forms. Chronic indigestion weakens the immune system, which reacts first with allergy, then with auto-immune disease, and finally with conditions in which immunity collapses altogether, like cancer or AIDS. Weakness of Ahamkara's self-identification with the body is the root cause of all such conditions." *Prakriti, Geocom Ltd., Albuquerque, NM; 1989, pg. 143*

Modern medicine will never be able to prevent or cure cancer and auto-immune diseases until they recognize the intelligent principle in both the universe and the body. It is this link that becomes damaged through denatured, processed food, poor life choices, emotional trauma, lack of love, ingestion of chemical medicines, and absorption of environmental chemicals. It is the intelligence that plays the key role between structure/form and system/functions. Yet, to say that this vision is the same concept as psychosomatic would be erroneous. The concept of psychosomatic relations and disorders is certainly a part of the intelligent principle as presented in Samkhya. Nevertheless, Samkhya is far larger than the concept of mind/body, which it contains, but is not limited to.

It is possible to relate the concept of psychosomatic disorders to the relation of Manas and Buddhi to Ahamkara. After all the Ahamkara relates to the manifestation through both Manas and Buddhi which control the five forms of reception and expression. As stated already the Ahamkara will naturally try to move into the manifestation – that is its proper role. Ultimately this is the cause of mental suffering that eventually leads to disease and death.

The Jiva residing in the Ahamkara never forgets its source of wholeness, or unity as the principle of Purusha. Therefore, when the Ahamkara moves into the manifestation and seeks to express itself through material objects, emotional relationships, or any form of sensory exchange, it is dissatisfied. This dissatisfaction comes from the inability to maintain pleasure through the sensory objects and relationships. At the most Ahamkara gains and experiences pleasure for brief periods of time as in sexual orgasm, eating, feeling love, and buying new items. However, this pleasure lasts from a few moments to hours, perhaps even days in some cases, but eventually it has to pass.

When the transient pleasure passes then there is dissatisfaction because the Jiva knows that it is by nature Being, Consciousness, Bliss (Satcitanand). This paradox of feeling our nature to be Bliss, yet only being able to experience Bliss (pleasure) for a short length of time, is the cause of all pain, anxiety, grief, depression, sorrow, suffering and dissatisfaction. This very sorrow or suffering causes the intelligence conscious principle (Jiva) to move away from the Ahamkara and weaken the link, or for it to move further into desires and sensual pleasures.

This is why Samkhya states that all disease is rooted in

Ayurvedic Relationships in Samkhya

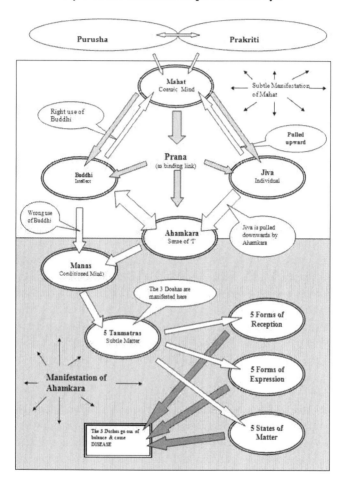

the diversification of Ahamkara from Mahat. In this process the Jiva continually longs for itself – for Satcitanand, Being, Consciousness, Bliss. This is the nature of the Jiva and is never lost. Each human being is pure consciousness – Purusha – by nature. Humans are the manifestation of Purusha and are not different from Purusha. True health according to Samkhya is to re-identify the Jiva/Prana with Purusha instead of the Ahamkara. This can only be done while alive and has no direct negative effect on the physical body.

The *Caraka Samhita*, one of Ayurveda's two oldest texts (prior to 1000 BC) states the following in the *Sutrasthana* section:

"The causes of disease relating to both mind and body relate to the wrong use of: time, mental faculties and sense objects. The wrong use is threefold: over utilization, no utilization and wrong utilization." I.54

"The body/mind are the substrata of both disease and health. A balanced utilization of time, mental faculties and senses results in health. A wrong or unbalanced use results in disease." I.55

"The Jiva is devoid of all pathogenic factors. The Jiva is the cause of consciousness in the body/mind and of the Tanmatras. The Jiva is eternal and observes all activities." I.56

The Caraka Samhita clearly indicates that the 'body/mind' is the basic cause of disease and that the Jiva, or individualized Purusha, is before and therefore free of disease.

In summary, the Samkhya states that disease is caused by a wrong use of intelligence (Buddhi) and by the wrong use of the senses. Hence, what we receive into the mind and express out through the mind are potential disease causing factors. Additionally, the root cause of all unhappiness and disease is the manifestation of the

Ahamkara, or 'individual principle'. Naturally the Ahamkara wants to move into the mental and sensual functions – the overuse or wrong use of which causes disease. Furthermore, the Jiva knows itself to be both eternal and blissful by nature. The paradox of feeling this and the inability to live it in the manifestation causes suffering and mental anxiety. The cure of which is to re-identify the individual with the causal factor of the universe – the Purusha or pure consciousness.

Thus, Samkhya gives us the fundamental vision of what causes disease and how we can both prevent disease and cure diseases like autoimmune disorders and cancer. In order to use this system as a transformational tool we may need to make fundamental changes in both our view and relation to life itself. The next chapter will propose some possibilities of how this can be feasible in daily life.

11
THE APPLICATION OF SAMKHYA IN DAILY LIFE

"For me there is no waking or dreaming, nor is there any posture of Yoga, nor is there any day or night. How can I say that I am in the third state (deep sleep) or in the Fourth (Turiya - transcendence)? I am by nature blissful and free." 4.17

The most fundamental mistake that can be made when approaching the psychology of transformation is to do so from an intellectual standpoint. The Samkhya system on which this method is based is first and foremost an experiential approach to understand and experience the universe. Approaching it simply from the intellect will cause misunderstandings and misinterpretations of the metaphors used to indicate the experiential reality of the universe.

The system itself was the result of direct observation. As stated earlier there are three classical methods of perceiving the universe around us. According to the ancient Vedic tradition from which Samkhya has come, direct perception is the highest form of knowledge.

The root of all perceptions for the human being

comes from Manas, the emotional and conditioned mind. From Manas the Tanmatras arise – the subtle link between the senses and the sense object. The Tanmatras are matter in a pure form – before they begin to interact and create form. On a subtle level this dimension relates to the astral planes or dream levels of manifestation. From the Tanmatras the five forms of perception arise, through these five sense organs we take in impressions from the world around us.

It is through the senses that we take in the impressions that condition the mind (Manas). According to Samkhya, the mind is a very sensitive organ that can be easily disturbed or traumatized by the impressions it receives. Things like car accidents, wars, murder, rape, and any form of mental violence, damage the sensitivity of the emotional, conditioned mind. Additionally, the mind, after receiving the information from the senses, interprets the information. This is the nature of the mind – to interpret or translate – the information received.

The emotional, conditioned mind then acts as a relay station between the outside world and the deeper levels of the mind – the intellect (Buddhi), the sense of 'I' or ego (Ahamkara), and the unconscious and subconscious minds (Chitta). All of these are influenced directly from the interpretations of Manas. This is one of the primary roles of Manas – to relay impressions and information to the other levels of the mind. This understanding of the four-dimensional mind does not exist clearly in Western psychology. Using this model we can penetrate to a deeper level of psychological understanding.

However, the weakness of Manas is that it interprets everything external according to its own conditioning. There is no other option open to Manas, the conditioned, emotional mind. This means that if I am a scientist I will tend to interpret the world – even personal relationships – from the conditioning of a logical, rational intellect. If I am an artist I will tend to interpret the universe as an expression of art and (hopefully) beauty. An athlete will tend to look at life from a competitive view and so on. In and of itself there is nothing wrong in this. Unfortunately the mind, once conditioned, cannot tell when it is appropriate to interpret one thing and not another.

A simple example is that which most modern people have experienced at least once or twice in their life – the confusion of the workplace with the home. On a professional level we are generally forced to behave in a certain manner, which is appropriate for our profession, be it window washing or management. However, humans often end up continuing to behave in the same manner at home with their spouse and children. This has been the cause of more than a few divorces. It is hard for the conditioned mind to change roles, and even harder to become aware of its own conditioning.

It is only through developing the higher side of Buddhi that Manas (conditioning) can be observed. If the Buddhi is not developed then self-observation becomes difficult or impossible. Stronger demands on the conditioned mind make it harder for the Buddhi to function on its higher, discriminative level. One example of this could be a managerial position that has tremendous responsibilities. These responsibilities force the individual to increase the strength of Manas out of survival. Slowly the individual will lose self-observation unless a conscious effort is made to develop it directly. This is why many CEO types are very difficult to be around on a personal level. It must be emphasized that the Samkhya term of Buddhi, which we loosely translate as 'intellect', is not the rational, logical intellect, but rather the feeling, discriminating fire of perception as described in the previous chapters.

Thus direct perception is impossible through Manas. It is also impossible through Buddhi. Direct perception can only be before the manifestation of Ahamkara. On the level of Mahat, the Cosmic Mind, direct perception can be known on a universal level of unity. On the level of

Prakriti, matter in potentiality, direct perception can be known as unity with matter itself. On the dimension of Purusha direct perception can be experienced as Being, Consciousness, Bliss, but not known. The method that we can use to get from Manas to Mahat is the Buddhi – even though Buddhi itself cannot directly perceive reality. So the real question is: "How to develop Buddhi?".

The answer lies in the source of all manifestation – Prakriti. Inherent in Prakriti are three attributes that actually form all of the creation. They are called Sattva, Rajas and Tamas as explained in chapter Three. From these three 'gunas' or attributes everything arises. The following diagram shows how the whole creation comes forth from these three attributes. In essence, all of the manifestation comes from the principle of Rajas or action. Without the basic principle of active movement the creation could not manifest. The main expression of Rajas is Prana as the cosmic energy of creation (Pranasakti) and secondarily, the five forms of expression, or five motor organs.

From the other two Gunas the manifestation arises in both subtle and solid forms. The Sattvic principle controls the mind and senses. The Tamasic principle controls the sense objects, the five states of matter and the resulting physical manifestation. These are the cosmic roles of the Gunas.

From these three primary qualities come the twenty attributes – the ten pairs of opposites – which allow us to use the creation in a practical way. In chapter Five these principles were introduced. They give us the means to use Ayurveda, Yogic psychology, astrology, Tantra and yoga in daily life. In Ayurveda all diagnosis and treatment is based on the dominant or deficient attribute. Likewise, in psychology the dominant attribute gives us a means to further refine the general indications of the primary Guna. In astrology the attributes tell us the qualities and actions of the planets in a chart. All of creation can be understood through the three primary Gunas and their sub-qualities the twenty attributes.

The Gunas, when in their proper roles, support creation and life. If for some reason they move out of their normal creative role they cause disease, death and destruction. The most sensitive of these domains is that of the fourfold mental functions – Buddhi, Ahamkara, Manas and Chitta. The whole mental functioning belongs to the attribute of Sattva, intelligence and purity. When either Rajas or Tamas begins to dominate in the mind then there begins to be disruption in the whole organism.

On an individualized level of manifestation – the dimension of Ahamkara, Buddhi and Manas (our psychology) – the three Gunas have the following attributes:

Sattva	Intelligence, flexibility, peace, intuition, clarity, happiness, self-love, compassionate, understanding, creativity, caring, humanitarian
Rajas	Action, dispersing, agitation, anger, jealousy, frustration, ego, overbearing, aggressiveness, loud, overuse of stimulants, violence, motivated, goal seeking, workaholic
Tamas	Inertia, inflexibility, dullness, stupidity, violence, perversion, depression, unhappiness, lack of love, drug addiction, delusions, insanity, deceiving, dishonesty

Sattva should be predominating in the mind, as that is its domain. When either Rajas or Tamas dominate then Manas becomes disturbed. Of the two Tamas is the most difficult because it obscures the ability of self-observation and honesty. It is quite common that a person with dominate Tamas thinks they are very Sattvic – I have observed this many times in both clients and students.

In modern society we are mentally a mix of the three Gunas. Our culture demands a Rajasic mentality and often we become fixed in ideas or emotions that indicate Tamas. The ancient methodology is to increase Rajas to move the

Samkhya and the Three Gunas

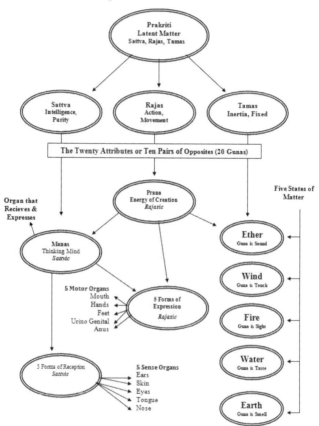

inert Tamas. A Tamasic mind cannot be changed directly – one has to use Rajas (dispersing action) to diminish the inertia of Tamas. Pure Sattva is basically unheard of today, as our culture does not support it. If someone is saying that they are predominately Sattva it usually indicates a dominance of Tamas or self-delusion.

It is also important to acknowledge that a dominance of Tamas does not mean that the person is violent or a pervert. It usually manifests as depression, lack of love, unhappiness or just blindness to one's real state. These are the most common mental problems of our culture and they are all related to Tamas. Alternatively high Rajas does not necessarily mean the person is an egoist and overbearing. The modern type 'A' person is classically Rajas. Over working and the inability to stop 'achieving' indicates very high Rajas. Usually violence is a combination of Rajas (action) and Tamas (delusion).

The Samkhya has demonstrated over and over that the development of Buddhi is a key factor in reversing the downward movement of creation. One of the primary ways to develop the higher discriminative powers of Buddhi is to promote Sattva in the mind. The predominance of Rajas gives one an analytical, logical, intellectual mind, but also one that is unfeeling and mechanical. Predominance of Tamas drives the Buddhi downward into Manas and sense pleasures, and the continual need for stimulation to activate the dullness of the mind.

Another key to developing the Buddhi is through the impressions we receive from our environment. If one is living in a violent neighborhood it tends to promote either fear or its opposite, violence. By the same token watching violent movies will increase your own anger, frustration and violence according to Samkhya. Eventually modern psychology will recognize the obvious truth of Samkhya that says what we receive into our sensitive mind conditions and forms its function. The increase of violent crimes among the young in relation to the increase of media violence is an obvious example.

Additionally, as the American media moves into other less violent cultures those cultures slowly become more violent. Western Europe is one example of the increase in crime over the last generation with the influx of Hollywood type media. Another is the increase of rape and sexual assault in India, traditionally a sexually conservative culture (at least in the last 1000 years).

Hence, the selection of what we allow into our senses will affect our mind. A man looking at pornography will always be thinking of sex. A woman looking at clothing catalogs will be often thinking of buying new clothes. A child watching TV and seeing the new toys will want to have the latest toy. These truths are exploited everyday by the American marketing machine which uses sex to sell refrigerators, clothes and thousands of other items (hopefully not toys!). One wonders sometimes if the marketing executives are not better psychologists than the psychologists themselves!

Limiting or choosing what is received into the conditioned mind (Manas) helps to promote Buddhi because the downward movement is lessened. This is important for our children as well. They should be given structure and time limitations with TV, computer, tablets and smart phones. There is already enough sense impressions through advertising on the street and shopping malls – one does not need to bring it into the home more than necessary.

Again it has to be emphasized that Samkhya is nonjudgmental and promotes freedom of choice at all times and on all levels. It also understands the effects of poor choices – but anyone is free to make them.

The psychology of transformation also recognizes that the intake of food affects the Gunas in the mind and so ultimately the Buddhi. The fundamental idea that the whole creation is inter-linked through Purusha / Prana means that food ingested on the most physical level will eventually affect Manas, Buddhi and Mahat. Modern research which began in the 1960's and still continues today shows that certain food additives change behavior of both children and adults. The first series of these studies were discounted in the media by a huge campaign from certain medical associations and the food industry itself. However, the science, the methodology and the conclusions themselves have never been proved wrong in vitro or in field studies during the last forty-five years. There is recent media awareness of the possible link of food to cancer and other serious diseases.

What we take into our bodies on the sense impression level conditions the psychology and what we take into our mouth conditions the metabolism. Hence a diet based on pure foods is one of the ways that psychology of transformation uses to promote the higher aspects of Buddhi, the intelligent principle of discrimination and self-observation.

The other side of this is the expression of the impression received. If we intentionally hurt or harm others – emotionally or physically – it pulls the Buddhi down into the lower sensual mind. Hence, expression is as important as reception. Often it can indicate the purity of mind and motivations of a person. On one hand expressions can be seen as the highest product of the whole creation. If they are creative and bring new knowledge or beauty to the world it is a means to develop Buddhi. If the expression is destructive, damaging and is against knowledge and beauty then it brings down Buddhi into a negative state.

Therefore, the practical things that we can do in life to preserve our health mentally and physically is to limit the intake of impressions and food to pure, healthy material. How we express ourselves is equally important on both a personal and social level. Additionally, we can strive to promote the higher ideals of humanity in our consciousness, which increases Sattva. These are fundamental steps for reversing the downward movement of creation. They are important and provide the foundation, but they represent the beginning.

If the Buddhi has the capacity of self-observation then the real adventure of going beyond the 'sense of I' or Ahamkara can be undertaken. Actually, one does not choose this – it happens naturally. If the desire to go beyond the Ahamkara arises then it is like a magnet that pulls one higher and higher in the creation of ideas, form, and concepts. It will happen many times that the individual will encounter the Cosmic Mind of Mahat and have numerous experiences of unity, love, peace and being. This is both beautiful and painful as it is still an experience and therefore transitory. Eventually all of humanity will return to its source of Pure Consciousness – it is only a question of time – that paradox which ends when the individual merges into the universal.

The unfathomable journey back to Purusha cannot be explained in a book. It requires such an individual approach that writing something on it would be meaningless as it would have relevance only to the author himself or herself. As far as this chapter can go in the explanation of re-identification with Purusha is to clarify the development of Buddhi and the possibility of moving beyond the concept of 'I' and the individual conditioning. Beyond this requires an individual approach in harmony with the person. However, once undertaken this adventure is truly the 'adventure of a lifetime'.

12

THE PSYCHOLOGY OF
TRANSFORMATION AS YOGA

"Renounce, renounce the mundane existence and then renounce completely even that renunciation. Give up like poison the egoistic idea of either shunning or accepting the world. You are the pure, simple, unchanging and immortal Self." 3.46

There is a practical method of psychological transformation that is based on the Samkhya system and Vedanta. This method is very effective and simple to explain and learn. The only problem is that it is very difficult to implement unless the concepts of the previous chapter are integrated in daily life.

Without the development of discrimination (the higher aspect of Buddhi) and the cultivation of Sattva (harmony and peace) in the mind this method is not possible to use. Or, if it is used then it can lead to self-delusion, as any lack of self-discrimination will. In short it is not a magic pill and relies on an integral approach to life. If this done according to the explanation of this book then it is very effective to bring lasting peace and happiness to all levels of the mental functioning.

To illustrate this method it is necessary to remember that the mental field of Manas is the receptor of all images received by the senses. Because of this function there arises the process of thinking. As the images from life are stored in memory these supply an unlimited source of thoughts. It is worthy to note that memory consists of three basic levels – Chitta for automatic functions (e.g., memory to breath), Manas for emotions (e.g., pleasure and pain) and Ahamkara for undigested experiences (e.g., suppressed or blocked). Thus, between the reception of images and stored images in memory thoughts are continuously present in Manas or mind.

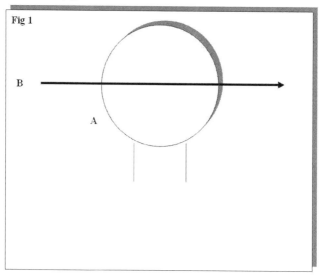

Fig 1

B

A

The problem is that we assume that these thoughts are like a freeway – several lanes of traffic that never stop. This is the first erroneous concept according to Vedantic psychology.

Figure 1. demonstrates this misconception. The round circle, or A, represents the head and generally our normal field of awareness. This is Manas (conditioned, emotional mind) unless some effort is made to use Buddhi the line remains solid. The solid line, or B, represents the idea that thoughts are a continious stream of unstoppable traffic. This view does not allow freedom for the indvidual and creates a vitcim or slave type of situation to the "rush hour traffic" flow of thoughts.

The view of the psychology of transformation is represented by Figure 2. In this diagram note the addition of C which represents the actual movement of thoughts. The difference is a major one in that each arrow represents a thought – meaning that each thought is an individual thing and so can be confronted or dealt with in some way. This allows for freedom and stops the victim mentality that all thoughts are one unstoppable flow.

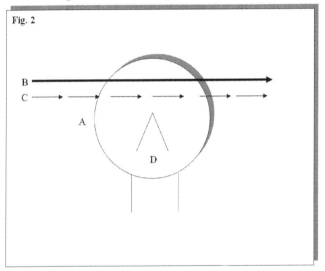

Fig. 2

Thus the dashed arrows of C show that each thought is an individual automobile on the highway. Both B and C have a definite movement through the mind as they follow the highway. The arrows themselves represent the highway as a direction and the automobiles that drive on it. This is how the flow of thoughts function in the mind. Close observation of the mind reveals the perpetual movement of thoughts. It can be experienced by trying to focus on one thought alone for several minutes. Generally it is difficult to hold one thought for more than 5 to 10 seconds because other thoughts move in and push it away.

The point of awareness is represented by D and an arrowhead in the field of A, or the mind. This indicates that only one thought at a time can pass over our awareness. This is also easily observable by trying to think of two things at once. If full attention is given it can be seen that only one thought can be observed at a time. The transition between two thoughts is often so fast that we don't notice it unless we use our full attention. This 'one pointed' quality of awareness is important as it gives us the freedom to pick and choose thoughts individually. It allows us to work with any thought or emotion. It is important to note that from the Samkhya point of view emotions and feelings are equally a part of Manas and so are not different from a thought. Emotions, thoughts and feelings are considered to be objects because they can be observed and managed in some way. We can observe all functions of Manas from the higher side of Buddhi, or discrimination. It is first the Buddhi who begins self-observation to develop self-awareness. If the person has spiritual motivations this Buddhi eventually merges back into its source of cosmic intelligence or Mahat.

Thus the arrowhead as shown by D represents the self-awareness that is developed with the function of Buddhi. This awareness is not Buddhi. It is consciousness or Jivatman and it becomes apparent with the development of Buddhi. Awareness can merge back into cosmic awareness if the person so desires. In any case this awareness is there because of the Jiva or our individual piece of Purusha and is the "substratum" of who we are. Usually we are not aware of it per se.

In normal everyday life the thoughts are moving though the awareness of Manas. Problems arrive only if one of these thoughts becomes stuck the field of awareness, or A, as shown in figures 1 and 2. When a thought becomes stuck in A we feel this as some sort of disturbance. Several examples are: stress, anxiety, worry, fear, anger, lust, jealousy, depression, insomnia, frustration, etc. Figure 3 shows how a single thought changes its normal direction and becomes trapped in the field of A, or the mind. These larger arrows move in a circular motion that keeps them ensnared in Manas. Hence, according to this approach of psychology it is the obsession with a trapped thought or emotion that is the causal factor behind all psychological disturbances and disorders. In order to stop mental disturbance the troublesome thought simply needs to be released and allowed to move out of the field of awareness of A.

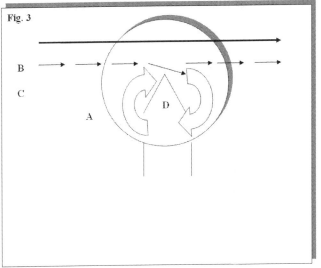

Fig. 3

In order to allow the thoughts or emotions to move out we need to understand how they have become entrapped in the first place. The main reason why the mind traps a thought is because there is an affinity to that thought or emotion. If there is no affinity then the thought simply passes out of the awareness without making any kind of impact. If there is an affinity the past memories create a relationship with the thought. Once the relationship is established the thought becomes trapped in the field of awareness or Manas.

Consequently, the first step to be free of psychological disturbance is to identify the affinity and relationship that results. Thus, identification is the primary step in stopping mental agitation. In this sense Western psychology is very useful as the primary function of this psychology is analytical and seeks to understand the nature of problems thought identification and classification. The principal difference between the two systems at this point is that the ancient Indian system is not concerned with the 'how' or 'why'. In fact, it is the obsession with the 'how and why' of past events that keeps the Manas constantly in a downward movement. This orientation prevents the higher aspects of Buddhi to develop and actually increases the power of the Ahamkara to pull the Manas downward into further creation.

The trick is to simply identify the problematic thoughts and not concern ourselves with the other aspects. Once we move into the memory and past we move into Manas and out of the higher side of Buddhi. If we stay obsessed with the 'how and why' of problems we remain a victim to the thought or emotion. We can only gain empowerment or freedom by staying in the present. The moment we turn ourselves to past and memory we become victims because no one has the power to change the past. We can only change the present.

Once the affinity and relationship have been identified we begin to have power – we begin to become free of the problem. The next step is to choose what we want – to stay in the trap of the thought and all the past it is invoking – or to leave it for the happier state of the present. My teacher Sri Poonjaji calls this the choice for peace. If there is no desire for peace and happiness then this method is useless. If on the other hand a person wishes truly to be peaceful then one has to make a strong decision for peace. The strength of the past is powerful and without a firm decision for peace it is very difficult to break past mental habits. Self-honesty is also important. Some things one may wish to leave as they are – concentrate on the issues that disturb the life the most.

At this moment after the decision for peace has been made we need to focus our awareness or attention – D in figures 2 and 3. Now it is simply a question of where we put our attention. If the attention stays with the entrapped thought then the thought gains power.

An example may help: You walk out of a store and begin to cross the street when a car almost hits you. Your mind is naturally in a slight state of shock. You curse the diver as being stupid – now according to your past experiences and memory the entrapment begins. If the driver was another gender then it could follow – "all men are reckless and stupid" or "crazy women driver". If the driver was of another race then one can fall into racial discrimination and generalization, such as "dam Laplander, they can only drive reindeer!". Or if you just had to meet with your lawyer for a court case you may think, "Idiot! Must have been a lawyer!"

After these initial thoughts we can either forget about it and cross the street or keep feeding the thoughts with our attention. The power of the mind to twist and turn events is actually quite normal and happens to each of us every day. This is because Manas is both receiving and then linking experiences and information together all day. The more Tamasic (dull) Manas is, the more extreme the seemingly arbitrary links are made in the mind.

Therefore, where we place our attention is extremely important. We have the choice and are responsible for our joy or unhappiness. This choice is simply a question of choosing where to place our attention on a daily basis. In the above example the person could eventually convince himself to attack (physically or psychologically) the car driver. On the other hand he could walk across the street and feel happy that he is still alive. The choice of how we react or respond to the thoughts and events in life is what makes us slaves or kings in life.

The most effective way to use attention is to catch affinities and relationships when they first begin – at the intersection of D with the thought. This is the most difficult at the beginning, but slowly becomes easy as we become familiar with the troublesome thought or emotional pattern. At first when we have identified a problematic thought we usually need some method of diverting the attention. Due to a lifetime of habit we generally are not used to moving or controlling where we put our attention.

There are two primary ways to divert attention. The first is mental, the second is physical. The physical is the easiest way as we can simple change an activity, like start cleaning the house to forget something, or go running, or swimming. Any physical activity will divert the attention temporarily. This is the drawback though – it is usually just a temporary diversion. The mental methods are usually more difficult, but longer lasting. Often a combination of the two is needed if a real problem comes up or one that is from the deeper conditionings of Manas.

It is important to clarify the term diversion of attention at this point. This is not to be confused with avoidance, repression or running away from a problem. According to this system feeding a thought is increasing the problem. What this system suggests is to consciously choose another approach to becoming free of the past memories and conditioning which make up Manas or the mind. When there is a clear conscious decision this is not avoidance or suppression. Nor is it positive thinking in which we simply block out other thoughts and focus only 'positive' thoughts.

Diversion of the attention is to free mental energy (*pranavayu*) so that it can go into Buddhi rather than into Manas. Normally our mental energy is so busy with the past memories and conditioning – in relation to the current experiences – that little or no energy is moving into Buddhi. Once Buddhi begins to receive energy the power of discrimination begins to develop and become active. This in turn provides the possibility to stop being a victim to learned behavior and old memories that normally dominate our waking state. The result of this method is an increase of happiness and contentment.

Another way to understand the affinity and relationship stage is through learned behavior. Manas is the conditioned mind and it subsequently learns everything – including how to act and respond. Thus, diverting the attention is a methodical technique to un-condition the learned behavior of the past. This conditioning is also comprised of memories as it is our past experience that conditions us.

Hence, diverting the attention is a fundamental way of empowering the individual. As stated several times in this book the Samkhya system – and therefore, Yoga, Ayurveda and Jyotish – firmly believe in free will and choice. One is free to choose peace and an upward movement into Pure Consciousness or free to move downward into sense gratification and indulgence with food, money, power and sex. Empowering the individual means to awaken the Buddhi to allow for an awakening of consciousness. In this sense it does not mean empowering the ego or lower aspect of Ahamkara.

To return to the two methods of diverting the attention we see that both are a means of re-leaning to use our conditioned minds. One could also say that this is a way to actually become an adult. If we are only living from our past memories and conditioning then we are, in fact, still living as children because our basic conditioning has been finished by the age of five years old. To take this to the level of Samkhya it means that we are reconditioning the mind to become human, as functioning only from Manas is the level of animals.

The physical method of diverting the attention is at best temporary. So what then are the options to divert the attention mentally? The first is directly through will power – simply decide not to think about, or get into a relationship with the questionable thought. The second is to substitute the problematic thought with something else. In the ancient Indian traditions Sanskrit syllables are used. These are called *bijamantras*, or 'seed sounds'. These sounds resonate in Manas and begin to harmonize the reception and expression of ideas. They are an active method so they are Rajas in nature. This is useful to change deep-seated patterns or mental habits, which are considered to be Tamas in nature. However, the mindless repetition of any sound will not bring happiness. It is necessary to be conscious of the habit, thought or conditioning in which you are consciously choosing to re-program.

Some schools or people advocate the repetition of bija mantras as a means of Self-realization. Sri Poonjaji has said a number of times that he has never seen any result from *Japa* or repetition of bija mantras concerning Self-Realization. He is in a good position to know as he spent more than 15 years doing up to 80,000 daily repetitions of *namajapa* per morning before work. Using bija mantra or single Sanskrit words like Hrim, Shrim, Klim, Kleem or Ram is definitely an aid to divert the awareness and break old mental habits in Manas. They help to awaken Buddhi and can turn Manas in an upward moving direction. They destroy Tamas and help to develop Sattva by activity (Rajas). They can help awaken deep-seated devotion to the divine - Bhakti or the path of love - in a person. But it is untrue that the repetition of a mantra will enlighten an individual. Mantra is a form of practice. The question of Self-realization is of identification not in adding more practice or concepts. Hence, using bija mantra is a valuable tool psychologically and also very important as a meditation method.

Using sound as means of diverting the attention is very useful and helps prepare the mind for the more direct and efficient method of directly rejecting the thought as it passes awareness or point D in figure 3. This is something like recognizing an unwanted guest and saying, "Oh my God, if I let them in they will be here for two hours and I won't have time to cook dinner....". As with the un-invited guest just don't open the door when they knock. You have the choice and only you can open the door to past thoughts and conditioning.

Once we stop opening the door the unwanted guest stops coming back. This may take some time depending on how well you know the unwanted guest. Usually when a thought is identified clearly and the process of diverting the attention begins it loses its power in a few months. Normally even stubborn thoughts quiet after three months. This is actually a short time considering you may have lived for forty years or more. Even if you are twenty it represents twenty years of conditioning, which if you don't change, means you will remain a 3 to 6 year child your whole life emotionally / mentally. Why continue to be a slave to the past? Why not re-condition the thinking process to those thoughts and emotions that bring peace?

One should also be aware that this method usually goes through layers. This means that after stopping the habitual domination of a thought or emotion another seed thought or emotion is discovered. A simple example is the need to be loved – probably the most basic human need that arises due to the apparent separation from Purusha. This seed emotion or thought is the cause of numerous emotional habits and tendencies. Hence, working on conditioning or emotional behavior will ultimately uncover this seed thought.

My teacher emphasized the need to choose peace, first in the mind and second in speech, third in actions. This creates an atmosphere of consciousness that harmonizes Manas, strengthens Buddhi and weakens the power of Ahamkara to move downwards into creation. This methodology of Vedantic psychology is very effective to cure depression, stress and general unhappiness. But as stated in the beginning of this chapter, it is only possible to implement when a whole sattvic lifestyle is embraced. It is important to work with qualified psychotherapists or psychiatrists if serious mental shock has occurred. This method is primarily for healthy persons (or normally neurotic people like myself!) and is not meant to replace modern psychology, rather it supplements it.

This method can also be applied in a negative manner. This means that instead of diverting the attention one can negate the thought. This works in the same way but through questioning problematic thoughts as they arrive at point D in figure 3. This is a mental level method that can be helped by first using sound or the bija mantras. It requires that the person identify the thought as in the 'positive' or diversion method. After identification of the problematic thought the person questions if this thought is useful or not. If not, it is rejected. If it is considered to be useful it is kept. This requires a strong discriminative Buddhi to accomplish. This process is continued until the seed thoughts are discovered. When the seed thoughts are examined they in turn lead to the basic question of self-identification. Examples of seed thoughts are: I am American, I am a man, I am a father, etc. These seed thoughts include huge blocks of conditioning and the rejection of them results in large segments of past social conditioning being removed. One should always choose to keep what is useful, the point is to become aware of the seed conditionings so that one is not functioning out of slavery or as a victim, but from consciousness itself.

This methodology leads to empowerment and internal peace. This does not affect the external world and trials and tribulations of life. It does not stop the movement of thoughts or create an empty mind. Instead it addresses how we as human beings respond to the world and our thoughts and emotions. And finally it addresses who we identify ourselves to be - the Ahamkara or Purusha.

The view of my teacher, Sri H.W.L. Poonjaji, is that one should find out directly how the identification with 'I' (Ahamkara) functions. His message was that there is no method or practice to discover the 'I' as it is our eternal nature. Poonjaji stated a number of times that all practice increases the identification with the mind and 'I'. It is only by no-teaching, no-method that our real nature of Self is reviled. But this is beyond the scope of the Samkhya and the psychology of transformation as it transcends the manifestation of mind and the universe as we perceive it.

"On three accounts searching and practice are foolishness and misleading. They are only the clever mind postponing Freedom. The first is that it creates a searcher. This re-enforces the concept of an individual sufferer that is separate from Freedom, and that Self is something "other" than that Here and Now.

The Second is the search. Searching is a distraction which causes postponement and endless, needless suffering. Searching promotes religions, traditions, and paths to be adhered to, which serve only to trap you deeper in illusion. The truth is only Here and Now, but the search says it is tomorrow.

The third account is that search creates an object to be found, and this can be the subtlest and most misleading trap. As you start a search you conceptualize what it is that you are searching for. Since the nature of Maya, of illusion, is that whatever you think, so it becomes. Whatever you think the goal to be you will attain it.

There is no doubt about this: As you think so it becomes. So because of your search you will create and then attain that which you think you are searching for! Any heaven or high spiritual state that you long to attain you will attain after you conceptualize and create it. Then you will rest satisfied in the trap thinking that you have attained your "heaven".

The Truth is beyond thought, concept, and conditioning and this Truth is what you are, and only the Truth is."

Sri H.W.L. Poonjaji, The Truth Is, page 365

Relationships in the Sankhya System

Sanskrit	Principle	Qualities	Gunas	Dimension	Planet	World	Chakra	Kundalini	Body	Sheath
Purusha	Latent Consciousness	Sat, Chit, Ananda	None	Pure Consciousness	Sun	None	None	None	None	None
Prakriti	Latent Matter	Sattva, Rajas, Tamas	3 Gunas – Sattva, Rajas, Tamas	Pure Creative Energy	Moon	None	None	Domain of Kundalini	None	None
Mahat	Cosmic Mind	Sat, Chit, Ananda, Sattva, Rajas, Tamas		Cosmic or Universal Unity	Jupiter + Saturn -	Heavens	7th Crown of Head		Causal	Bliss Sheath
Ahamkara	Principle of Individuality	Diversification, Sense of 'I'		Jiva or Soul, Time & Space	Ascendant	Hells	3rd Navel		Subtle	Intellectual Sheath
Buddhi	Individual Mahat	Discrimination, Sensitive, Logic Reason, Intellect		Higher Mind	Mercury		6th Between the Eyebrows			
Manas	Individual Mind	Prana, Tejas, Ojas		Lower Mind, Includes Chitta	Moon		4th Center of Chest			Emotional Sheath
Tanmatras	Subtle Matter	Vata, Pitta, Kapha		Energetic, the 5 Pranas	Venus	Astral & Earth	4th Center of Chest			Pranic or Etheric Sheath
Pancha Jnanendriyani	5 Forms of Reception	Sound Touch, Sight, Taste, Smell		Feeling	Venus		2nd Top of Pubic Bone			
Pancha Karmendriyani	5 Forms of Expression	Speech, Holding, Motion, Emission, Elimination	Manifest through the 20 Attributes	Expressing	Mars	Earth	5th Base of Throat			
Pancha Mahabhutani	5 States of Matter	Space, Movement, Transformation, Cohesion, Solid		Solid Matter Manifested, Form	Saturn	Earth	1st Perineum		Physical	Physical Sheath
Prana	Intelligent Movement	Intelligent, Binding, Energy	Chala or Movement	Links all Dimensions	Sun / Mars	Links all Worlds	Energy of Transformation	Udana Prana (Shakti)	Links all Bodies	Links all Sheaths

124

BIBLIOGRAPHY

Advaita Bodha Deepika, trans., Swami Ramanananda,
Tiruvannamalai, India: Sri Ramanasramam, 1990
Atreya, Ayurvedic Healing for Women, York Beach, ME:
Samuel Weiser, 1999
_____, Perfect Balance: Ayurvedic Nutrition for Mind,
Body and Soul, New York, NY: Avery Publishing,
2001
_____, Practical Ayurveda: Secrets of Physical, Sexual &
Spiritual Health, York Beach, ME: Samuel Weiser,
1998
_____, Prana: The Secret of Yogic Healing, York Beach,
ME: Samuel Weiser, 1996
_____, Secrets of Ayurvedic Massage, Twin Lakes, WI:
Lotus Press, 2000
Avadhuta Gita, trans., Swami Chetanananda, Calcuta,
India: Advaita Ashrama, 1995
Bhagavadgita, trans., Swami Gambhirananda, Calcuta,
India: Advaita Ashrama, 1991
Caraka Samhita, trans., Dash, Dr. Bhagwan & Sharma, Dr.
R.K., Varanasi, India: Chowkamba Series Office,
1992, 5 vols.
Caraka Samhita, trans., Kaviratna, Dr. A.C. & Sharma, Dr.

P., Delhi, Inida: Sri Satguru Pub., 1996, 5 vols.

Nisargadatta Maharaj, I Am That, Bombay, India: Chetana Ltd., 1991

_____, Prior To Consciousness Durham, NC: Acorn Press, 1985

_____, Seeds Of Consciousness, Durham, NC: Acorn Press, 1990

_____, Consciousness And The Absolute, Durham, NC: Acorn Press, 1994

Pancadasi, trans., Vidyaranya Swami, Madras, India: Ramakrishna Math, 1987

Poonja, Sri H.W.L., The Truth Is, York Beach, ME: Samuel Weiser, 1999

Ramana Maharishi, Be As You Are, Ed. David Godman, New Delhi, India: Penguin Books India, 1992

_____, Talks With Sri Ramana Maharishi, trans. Swami Ramanananda, Tiruvannamalai, India: Sri Ramanasramam, 1984

Svoboda, Dr. Robert, & DeFouw, Hart, Light on Life, New York, NY: Penguin Books, 1996

Tripura Rahasya, trans., Swami Ramanananda, Tiruvannamalai, India: Sri Ramanasramam, 1989

Upanishads -

Brhadaranyaka Upanishad, trans., Swami Madhavananda, Calcuta, India: Advaita Ashrama, 1997

Chandogya Upanishad, trans., Swami Gambhirananda, Calcuta, India: Advaita Ashrama, 1992

Eight Upanishads, vols. I & II, trans., Swami Gambhirananda, Calcuta, India: Advaita Ashrama, 1992

Svetashvatara Upanishad, trans., Swami Gambhirananda, Calcuta, India: Advaita Ashrama, 1995

Yoga Vasistha, "The Supreme Yoga" Vols. I & II, trans., Swami Venkatesananda, Shivanandanagar, Uttar Pradesh, India: Divine Life Society, 1991

GLOSSARY

Agni: another name for Chit, the cosmic principal – as in sat, chit, ananda; quality of Purusha; god of fire; digestive fire.

Ahamkara: the principle of individuality; diversification; sense of 'I'

Atman: pure consciousness, Purusha.

Ayurveda: The oldest medical system in the world. A holistic approach developed by the same sages who formed the systems of yoga. The part of the Vedas dealing with the health of the body; 'the science of life'.

Brahma: the creator or creative aspect or Prakriti as a deity; the founder of Ayurveda in the form of a god.

Brahman: another name for Purusha; a term used to describe that which is not possible to describe, it is often just called - being, conscious, bliss, or sat, chit, ananda.

Brahmin: the learned class of people in Vedic society; priests.

Bramhacharya: abidance in Brahma or the un-manifest reality Purusha.

Buddhi: individual intellect; discrimination, sensitive intellect.

Caraka Samhita: the oldest surviving text of Ayurveda; one of the three ancient Ayurvedic texts of medicine.

Chit: unconscious, or subconscious mind; consciousness as part of Purusha.

Consciousness: as used in this book, Purusha or Source of all manifestation.

Dosha: three intelligent forms of prana that control the mix of matter in biological manifestations; lit: that which will imbalance or 'fault'; Vata, Pitta, Kapha.

Expression: five forms of expression; five organs of action; speech, holding, motion, emission, elimination

Five elements: Five States of Matter; the states of material existence: mass, liquidity, transformation, movement, and the field in which they function; also called: earth, water, fire, air, & ether (space).

Five states of matter: see Five Elements.

Guna: quality, attribute of Prakriti; there are three gunas: sattva, rajas, and tamas; also there are 20 sub-gunas that come in ten pairs of opposites.

Guru: Literally means 'dispeller of ignorance'; one who knows the substratum or source of creation.

Inquiry: method to find out where the 'I' thought arises from; question: "Who am I?"; see books of Ramana Maharishi, Nisargadatta Maharaj and H.W.L. Poonjaji.

Jiva: individual aspect of Purusha when Ahamkara manifests, also called Jivatman; soul.

Jivatman: see Jiva.

Jyotish: Vedic Astrology; 'science of light'; science of time and astronomy.

Kapha: one of the three doshas; controls water and earth elements.

Karma: action; the cosmic law of 'cause and effect'; there is no such thing as "bad or good" karma; therapeutically it is the general action of a substance on the body.

Kundalini: the primordial prana that rests dormant in the body unless activated by special practices; NOTE: these practices are dangerous unless one is supervised by a qualified teacher.

Latent Impressions: in Sanskrit there are two kinds: Vasanas & Samskaras, these are latent, unconscious or stored impressions and current mental impressions; they are the result of action (karma); these impressions are stored in the subtle body; these impressions are what cause us to incarnate in another life, unless they are allowed to surface to consciousness; these impressions along with prana create what we call mind and bind the Ahamkara to the Jivatman).

Life Force: another name of prana

Mahat: Cosmic Mind; principle of unity manifested; cosmic intelligence; has the qualities of both Purusha and Prakriti

Manas: emotional or conditioned mind; can refer to all of the mind in general; one of four aspects of the mind – with Ahamkara, Chitta and Buddhi; Prana, Tejas, Ojas manifest here.

Mantra: the science of sound; by using the correct sound each prana can be harmonized - and so can Manas, the conditioned mind.

Maya: the illusion that everything exists as separate from Purusha.

Mind: Manas; the organ of Ahamkara; thoughts moving through consciousness, giving the illusion of continuity; the combination of prana, Jiva and vasanas.

Moksha: liberation; re-identifying with Purusha instead of Ahamkara.

No-Mind: non movement of thought; complete awareness; not to be confused with the Absolute, the individual still exists at this point, it is an aspect of Mahat; a state of mind.

Ojas: subtle aspect of Kapha dosha in the Manas and Ahamkara

Parabdha: the karma or action that is residual; the karma's in association with the body/mind manifestation, in other words as long as you have a body the Parabdha karma continues.

Pitta: one of the three Doshas; controls fire and water elements.

Prakriti: Latent Matter: creative principle in creation; the dynamic energy of consciousness; Mother Nature.

Prana: pra = before, ana = breath; the vital force; it arises from substratum of pure consciousness with Purusha as intelligence (agni) and love (soma) together they create the individualized consciousness – these three principles are also called sat, chit, ananda. There are five major pranas in the human body, prana, apana, samana, udana and vyana, they arise from the Tanmatras and the rajas guna.

Purusha: Latent Consciousness; the source of creation; un-manifest aspect of consciousness; the void.

Reception: five forms of reception; five sense organs; sound, touch, sight, taste, smell.

Rajas: one of the three gunas of Prakriti; principle of energy and dispersion in the creation; action, movement, bright, energy, aggression, aggravated mind, achievement, and strong emotions.

Samsara: the concept that we are separate from Purusha; suffering; illusion.

Samskaras: Innate energetic impressions that result from karma, see latent impressions.

Sattva: one of the three gunas of Prakriti; principle of harmony, purity and balance; the pure mind is called sattva; purity, peace, calm, beauty, happiness, quite obedient mind, and stable emotions.

Self: another name for pure consciousness or Purusha; also called Brahman or the substratum of all duality- i.e., creation; the same consciousness (Purusha) in all things, hence the term -"self".

Sakti: (Śākti) pure energy or prana; pure matter or Prakriti.

Siva: (Śiva) pure consciousness, Purusha; one of the three aspects of consciousness as god, the destroyer as manifested in Mahat.

Soma: another word for Ananda (bliss); nectar; the most subtle essence of ojas and kapha; the God Soma signifies love, unity.

Substratum: source of Purusha

Tejas: manifests as the higher level of Buddhi; the power of discrimination in the mind; the subtle form of pitta; part of the trinity –prana, tejas, ojas which is part of Ahamkara/Manas/Buddhi.

Tanmatras: Subtle Matter; cause of perception; matter before it begins to interact, the division of prana into five forms; link between seer and object – the act of seeing.

Tantra: A path that totally accepts all aspects of the physical world, believing that all things lead to the divine; worship of the divine mother; often confused as a sexual practice.

Tamas: one of the three gunas of Prakriti; principle of mass, inertia and darkness; inertia, dull, depressed, void, stupid, lazy, despair, and self-destructive emotions.

Vikriti: that which covers Prakriti or the manifestation itself.

Vasanas: see latent impressions.

Vata: one of the three Doshas; controls wind (air) and ether (space) elements.

Vedas: Literally it means knowledge, but used here to mean the Book of Knowledge, the oldest book in the world; there are four Vedas.

Vedic: means knowledge that come from the Vedas

Vishnu: consciousness as pure love; the aspect of consciousness that protects and preserves the world; as a god which manifests with Mahat he has seven main manifestations of which Rama and Krishna are the two most famous.

Yoga: Union; that which leads one back to the original source or Purusha; generally understood to mean a path or a practice leading to the Divine; not limited to Hatha yoga or asanas.

Vaidya Atreya Smith

ABOUT THE AUTHOR

Vaidya Atreya Smith was born in Santa Monica, California in 1956 and began meditation at the age of seventeen. He was a follower of Neem Kroli Baba, as well as Ram Dass, Alan Watts and other Western teachers from the mid 1970's. Atreya studied with the American Vedanta Society in Portland, Oregon in the late 1970's to early 1980's. He then joined a spiritual community in 1982 and lived in this group until 1991 when he met his current teacher Sri H.W.L. Poonjaji who gave him the name Atreya according to Indian tradition. He has lived in India for more than six years from 1987 to 1994.

Atreya Smith is the author of six books published in nine different languages on the art of Indian medicine and healing. He has also either written or edited four textbooks on Ayurveda for Western students. Since 1998 he directs the European Institute of Vedic Studies, Switzerland and where he continues to run an e-learning course for serious students all over the world. From 1987 he has studied with a number of Indian professors of Ayurveda in India. He continues his studies with his teachers in India.

He has a BSc in Biology and in 2005 was awarded the title of Vaidya (knower of Ayurvedic texts) in Varanasi for his work in Ayurveda. Since 1987 Atreya works as a professional healthcare practitioner working with thousands of patients in countries of Europe. He is a professional herbalist and the member of several professional organizations. He is also trained in Jyotish (Vedic astrology). He currently lives in the South of France with his wife where he prefers to enjoy a slower lifestyle and good, homemade food!

35083051R00083

Made in the USA
Lexington, KY
29 August 2014